# MAINFRÄNKISCHES MUSEUM

Fortress Marienberg Würzburg

## Guide to the Exhibits

With 46 pictures
and a diagram of the lay-out

4th edition 1987

### English text by Ilonka Schneider

Stürtz Verlag Würzburg

ISBN 3 8003 0305 1

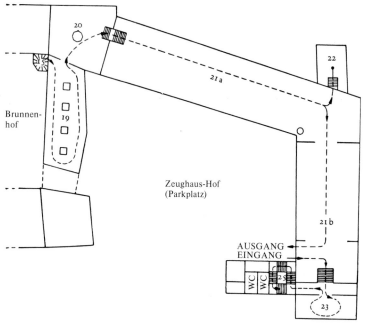

## Ground Floor

21b Entrance and
    Schönborn Hall
23  Church Room
25  Staircase
71  (between floors)
    Toilets
15  Winding Stairs

19  Lower Bulwarks
    (prehistoric exhibits)
20  Lower South Bulwark
    (romanesque sculptures)
21a Wine Press Hall
22  Casemate
21b Schönborn Hall
    and Exit

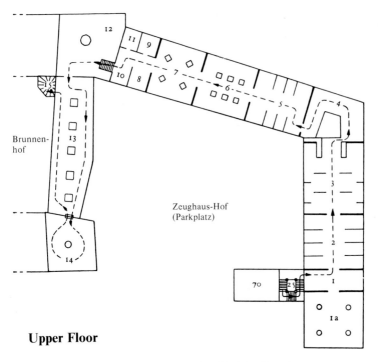

Brunnen-hof

Zeughaus-Hof
(Parkplatz)

## Upper Floor

1 Anteroom
1a "Stein" Room
2 Art Gallery
3 Riemenschneider Room
  (gothic sculpture)
4 Showcase Corridor
5 Pictures of Würzburg
6 Handicrafts Room
7 Garden-Room
8 Rococo Chamber
9 Tapestry Room
10 Corridor

11 Gothic Chamber
12 Knights' Hall
13 Central Bulwark
14 St. Kilian's Room
15 Winding Stairs
16/17/18 & a, b, c, d
    Folk Art
    (not shown in plan:
    entrance via the
    winding stairs 15)
70 Town-Model Room

# The Mainfränkische Museum

is an institution of the city of Würzburg but it is more than just a collection of exhibits pertaining to the history of the city, it is – as the name reveals – the provincial museum of Lower Franconia, and furthermore the historical museum of the former Bishopric of Würzburg and Dukedom of Franconia. It was founded in 1913 and was based on the collections of the Historical Society, the Franconian Art and Archeological Society and the City of Würzburg. Until 1939 it was known as the "Fränkische Luitpold Museum". The original 19th century building located in the city was destroyed when incendiary bombs sent the entire city up in flames on March 16th, 1945. In 1946 the museum was relocated up on the Marienberg in the very fortress that, for nearly five centuries, had served the Prince-Bishops of Würzburg and the Dukes of Franconia as a Residence. A wealth of significant works of art are housed here in the spacious rooms of the arsenal, which was partly destroyed by fire in 1945 and rebuilt between 1947 and 1951, and also in the impressive vaults of the Echter Bulwarks, which were restored from 1950 to 1954 for the use of the museum.

A multifarious collection of the works of artists and craftsmen, either born in Franconia or working here, and created by them in the course of centuries, are on display here and bear witness to the great epochs of art in this area.

In former times the museum was but one of the many sights worth seeing in the old yet intact city of Würzburg. With its sizeable number of exhibits which survived the war and its numerous valuable new exhibits the museum has become a virtual treasure chest of the resurrected city of Würzburg and at the same time a veritable "show-room" inviting lovers of art from all over the world to take a look at Franconia's great past and the fateful as well as the magnificent times of its capital city. Should the eye of the visitor to the new museum happen to stray away from the many works of art surrounding him and should he then glance out of the windows of the castle and look out across the sundrenched Main Valley he will come to appreciate more fully Würzburg's old yet unchanged function as crowned head of this richly endowed landscape.

It is the purpose of this guide to give the visitor to the museum a general idea of the exhibits and the rooms in which these are on display. Therefore only those exhibits which are of special importance are referred to in every room, whereby no claim to completeness is laid as far as the determination of what exactly is to be considered beautiful, valuable or important is concerned.

A black dot ● in front of the name of an item means that it is an exhibit of particular importance. Exhibits pertaining to the history of the city and state will soon find a spacious "home" in the beautifully situated upper floor of the Duke's Residence (town wing) in the Fortress with its expansive view of Würzburg and the Main River with its valley. In 1938 an exhibition of the town's history was already on view here but unfortunately it was destroyed in 1945.

Special exhibitions, the lending of exhibits to other museums and renovation or structural changes to the buildings sometimes make changes in the exhibits mentioned in the following tour inevitable.

### Arsenal and Echter Bulwarks

The present "home" of the museum is the former arsenal of the Fortress which was built during the reign of Prince-Bishop Johann Philipp von Greiffenclau on the initiative of the Chamberlain and Privy Counciller Jacob von Hohlach, by the engineer and architect Andreas Müller, teacher of the famous Balthasar Neumann. Balthasar Esterbauer created the Prince-Bishop's coat of arms which is to be found on the front of the building.

Directly adjacent, to the east, are the Echter Bulwarks, now also part of the museum. Erected in 1605 as the westernmost defences of the Fortress according to plans made by the Nuremberg architect Jacob Wolff the Elder for Prince-Bishop Julius Echter von Mespelbrunn.

# Tour

---

## Schönborn Hall (21 b)

with its great baroque ceiling and magnificent, spacious stairway contains several important works of art which are referred to at the end of the tour. Every year various "Museum Concerts" take place here. The ticket office and cloakroom are located under the gallery; postcards and books are also sold here.

*On the pillars:* ● Allegorical representation of morning, midday, evening and night in the shape of four putti (1766/67) taken from the garden of the former Prince-Bishops' summer residence in Veitshöchheim near Würzburg, made by Ferdinand Tietz (1708–1777), the court sculptor of Würzburg and Bamberg. (On loan from the Bayerische Verwaltung der Staatlichen Schlösser, Gärten und Seen).

*Carved doors (about 1790) by Peter Meckel*　　　7

*Opposite the entrance:* Portrait of Johann Philipp von Schönborn (1606–1673), Archbishop of Mainz, Prince-Bishop of
Würzburg and portrait of Friedrich Karl von Schönborn
(1674–1746), Prince-Bishop of Würzburg and Bamberg,
painted in 1729 by Johann Adam Remela (died 1740). Underneath – richly ornamented sandstone garden bench from Veitshöchheim by Ferdinand Tietz, about 1765. Further, portraits
of Cardinal Damian Hugo von Schönborn, Prince-Bishop of
Speyer and Constance (1676–1743), of Johann Philipp Franz
von Schönborn, Prince-Bishop of Würzburg (1673–1724) who
began the building of the Prince-Bishop's Residence in Würzburg, and of the Elector of Trier, Franz Georg von Schönborn
(1682–1756).

*Outside staircase:* The beautiful balustrade was brought here
from the cellar of the arsenal in 1950 while the stairs were
being built and extended by adding on a gallery. Two statues
of women saints (South German) from about 1750 stand at
the foot of the stairs. On the balustrade are two angel-putti
from Würzburg by Johann Peter Wagner (1730–1809), about
1780.

*On the gallery:* ● Carved doors from a house in Würzburg
done by Peter Meckel (1736–1805), about 1790. Beyond that
is the church room (23). Large portraits in richly carved frames
of Emperor Joseph II (1741–1790) and Empress Maria Theresia (1717–1780), painted in 1774 by the Viennese court painter
Joseph Hickel (1736–1807) for a Franconian castle.

## Church Room (23)

*Opposite the entrance:* ● Panel paintings of a winged altar-piece
possibly originating from Schlüsselfeld, painted by the so-
called "Master of the Hersbruck Altar" – an anonymous
painter from Bamberg, about 1485 (On loan from the Bayerische Nationalmuseum in Munich). Top left – "Christ on the

**8**

*So-called "Master of the Hersbruck Altar", "Presentation of Christ by Pilate", about 1485*

9

Mount of Olives", on the back – "Zacharias in the Temple"; bottom left – "The Scourging of Jesus at the Pillar", on the back – "Christening of John the Baptist". On the wall – "The Apprehension of Christ". Bottom right – "The Crowning with Thorns", on the back – "The Baptism of Christ". On the wall – "Presentation of Christ by Pilate". In the middle – the figures of two unidentified saints by a Franconian artist, about 1515.

*To the right of the entrance:* Two panel paintings belonging to the same altar "The Martyrdom of St. Kilian and his Companions" as well as "Miracle at the Body of St. Kilian" (On loan from the Bayerische Nationalmuseum Munich).

*Showcase on the wall, right-hand side:* plaster-cast copy of the face of the crucified Christ from the Cross located at one time in the chancel arch of the Cathedral of Würzburg, made after Tilman Riemenschneider (about 1460–1531) probably by Andreas Halbig (1807–1869) about 1850/60. Fragment of a Pietà made of burned clay, unknown artist, about 1410/20.

*End wall to the right:* ● Large panel painting "St. Agatha and St. Dorothy", from the former high altar of the parish church in Gerolzhofen, Franconian artist, about 1505/10. A further panel painting, "St. Valentine", Swabian artist, about 1530.

*In the window recess of the end wall on the right:* Two panel paintings "Enthroned St. Catherine" and "Enthroned Virgin with Child", South German artist, 1497. St. Anne, the Virgin and the Child (Anna Selbdritt), statue from the Riemenschneider-school, about 1520/30.

*In the window recess on the right:* Coloured statue of St. John the Apostle from a Crucifixion group, an early work by Tilman Riemenschneider, about 1490. Panel painting "St. Bartholomew", Würzburg artist, about 1475.

*In the window recess on the left:* Figure of Christ as the Man of Sorrows, Riemenschneider's workshop, about 1500.

End wall to the left: ● Panel paintings "Birth of Christ" and

"Adoration of the Magi", Franconian artist, about 1510 (On loan from the Bayerische Staatsgemäldesammlungen Munich).

*In the right-hand showcase, end wall on the left:* small gothic sculpture – Enthroned Virgin with Child, Swabian artist, mid-15th century; unidentified woman saint, Franconian artist, second half of the 15th century; St. Sebastian, Riemenschneider's sphere of influence, about 1510.

*In the left-hand showcase on the end wall on the right:* small gothic sculpture – Twin Madonna, Franconian artist, 2nd half

*Johann Peter Wagner, Lion with the coat of arms of Prince-Bishop Adam Friedrich von Seinsheim, about 1770*

of the 14th century (colouring of one side of the statue dates from the 19th century; new iron ring). Enthroned Virgin with Child from Iphofen, Franconian master, 13th century.

*To the left of the entrance:* ● Three panel paintings by a Franconian artist – "The Crucifixion", "Jesus is Placed in the Sepulcher", "Christ in Limbo". A further panel painting by the same artist "Farewell of the Disciples", about 1490.

*The ceiling of the room:* Madonna – candelabra, cast brass, Franconian artist, 1st half of the 17th century, from the Church of St. Burkart in Bad Kissingen.

## Staircase (25)

Pictures of commanders and officers of the Fortress during the baroque era. Among these – Portrait of the Würzburg Prince-Bishop's captain-engineer and architect, Andreas Müller, builder of this arsenal, painted about 1715 by Johann Adam Remela (died 1740). Sandstone Madonna from a Würzburg house, about 1725 by Balthasar Esterbauer (1672–1728). Lion with the coat of arms of the Prince-Bishop of Würzburg and Bamberg Adam Friedrich von Seinsheim (1708–1779), taken from the former shooting gallery, about 1770, by Johann Peter Wagner (1730–1809). Portrait of the Würzburg Prince-Bishop Johann Philipp von Greiffenclau (1652–1719), building sponsor of the arsenal, by the Würzburg court painter, Georg Franz Mika (1673–1749). Portrait of the Würzburg Chamberlain and Privy Councillor, Jacob von Hohlach, responsible for the construction of the new arsenal, painted by Georg Franz Mika, about 1715. Sandstone Madonna with Child from the façade of a Würzburg house, created about 1690 by Johann Kaspar Brandt (1652–1701).

Massive balustrade railing, constructed and installed in 1957 after an old Franconian model.

On the first floor to the left

**Anteroom of the Model Room (70)**
**in the former garrison headquarters**

*In the large showcase next to the entrance:* Weapons and suits of armour from the 12th–17th centuries. Among them – helmet and leg-armour of the so-called "Maximilian's coat of armour", early 16th century. Two half-suits of armour, about mid-17th century (On loan from the Germanische National-museum Nuremberg).

*Next to the showcase:* Shield, so-called "Pavese", with the coat of arms of Bamberg, about 1480.

*In two small showcases:* Two harnesses, 1st half of the 16th century.

*Between the windows:* Bronze arquebus with the coat of arms of the town of Gerolzhofen, 1545. A bronze gun-barrel, so-called "Serpentine", breech-loading device and coat of arms of the Lords of Schaumberg, about 1600. Bronze arquebus, with the coat of arms of the Würzburg Prince-Bishop Konrad von Thüngen (about 1466–1540) and the coat of arms of the Würzburg Chapter of the Cathedral, about 1530.

*Town Model "Würzburg about 1525"*      **13**

*In a wall showcase:* ● Three Würzburg executioners' swords with their sheaths, about 1500, 1534 and 1550.

Furthermore, halberds dating from the 16th of 17th centuries, including two weapons with the crest of the Würzburg Prince-Bishop Julius Echter von Mespelbrunn (1545–1617), late 16th century. Large partisan with etched decoration and the crest of the Archbishop of Mainz and Würzburg Prince-Bishop Johann Philipp von Schönborn (1605–1673). Three weapons bearing the crest of the Würzburg Prince-Bishops Christoph Franz von Hutten (1673–1729), Friedrich Karl von Schönborn (1674–1746) and Adam Friedrich von Seinsheim (1708–1779).

*On the right between the windows:* Four partisans with etched decoration and bearing the crest of the town of Würzburg, 17th century.

## Model Room (70)
## in the former garrison headquarters

● The large carved wooden model "Würzburg about 1525" (on a scale of 1:500) has been on display here since 1967. A donation of two Würzburg residents, the model was created between 1953 and 1963 by the two sculptors, Georg Achatz and Karl Steinbauer, according to the topographical charts and drawings of Dr. h.c. Franz Seberich (whose portrait painted by Heiner Dikreiter (1893–1966) hangs above the left-hand door of this room). The model shows the minutely detailed and fascinating panorama of this city in the late Middle Ages in all its splendour. Especially the eras of Bishop Rudolf von Scherenberg (1400–1495) and of Bishop Lorenz von Bibra (1456–1519) are vividly brought to life.

For the sake of comparison, views of 17th and 18th century Würzburg can be seen along the perimeter as well as the large depiction of the city after its destruction on 16th March 1945 by Willi Greiner (1898–1986).

*Joseph Anton Glantschnigg, Allegorical presentation of the Continents of Europe and Asia, about 1745*

## Anteroom (1)

*By the entrance:* Oil painting "Vulcan at the Forge of the Würzburg Court Locksmith Johann Georg Oegg" painted about 1750 by Joseph Anton Glantschnigg (1695–1755).

*On the left:* A scene from the orangery with the allegorical presentation of the Continents of Europe and Asia painted by the same artist, about 1745. Richly ornamented stone garden bench from Seehof Palace, the former Prince-Bishops' summer residence near Bamberg, by Ferdinand Tietz, about 1752.

*On the right:* A scene from the orangery with the allegorical presentation of the Continents of Africa and America by Joseph Anton Glantschnigg, about 1745. Carved Franconian console table, about 1750.

*In the middle:* Four putti by the court sculptor, Johann Peter Wagner (1730–1809). Taken from the terrace of the former

**15**

Prince-Bishops' summer residence in Veitshöchheim near Würzburg, 1776/77 – (On loan from the Bayerische Verwaltung der Staatlichen Schlösser, Gärten und Seen).

*On the left:* Two small scenes from the Old Testament by Johann Zick (1702–1762) "Jacob's Blessing" and "The Healing of the Blind Tobias". Between them a painting by Georg Anton Urlaub (1713–1759), "Joseph is pushed into the pit by his brothers", 1756. Richly carved console table made by Valentin and Georg Adam Schall about 1765, from Pfaffendorf Castle in the Baunach area.

*Near the window:* Oil sketch by Januarius Zick "The Miracle of Pentecost", design for a ceiling fresco in the parish church of Zell near Riedlingen, 1780.

*On the end wall:* Large mirror from the castle at Ellrichshausen on the Jagst, about 1760.

*On the right:* Two oil paintings "The Assumption" and "The Miracle at Pentecost" painted by an unknown Franconian artist, about 1765. Between these two, a painting by Georg Anton Urlaub "Joseph welcomes his brothers in Egypt", 1757. An intricately carved console table by Valentin and Georg Adam Schall, from Pfaffendorf Castle in the Baunach area, about 1765.

**To the right: "Stein" Room (1 a)**

So called because of the beautiful view of the vineyards on the Steinberg.

The 19th century paintings exhibited here are partly the work of Franconian artists, including several members of the Geist family, as well as the work of artists active in Franconia, such as Peter von Heß, the famous historical painter from Munich, and especially Ferdinand von Rayski dating from his Franconian period in 1837/38.

*To the left of the entrance:* Oil painting "Boatsmen on the Main River" painted in 1834 by Heinrich Ambros Eckert (1807–1840). ● Large historical painting by Peter von Heß

*Peter von Heß, "Laying of the Corner-Stone of the Constitution Monument near Gaibach", 1822/23*

(1792–1871), painted in 1823. It depicts the laying of the corner-stone of the Constitution Monument near Gaibach in 1821 by Crown Prince Ludwig of Bavaria, the later King Ludwig I, and Franz Erwein Count von Schönborn, who had the monument erected by the architect, Leo von Klenze, in commemoration of the first Bavarian constitution which was issued in 1818. In the centre, Crown Prince Ludwig and Count Schönborn, in the background Crown Princess Therese and Countess Emilie zu Castell-Castell. The remaining important personages can be identified with the help of the accompanying portrait sketch, below the picture made in 1821. Chest of drawers, probably Franconian, influenced by the workshop of David Roentgen, about 1790.

*Near the window on the left:* Portrait of Ludwig I of Bavaria (1786–1868) as Crown Prince, painted in pastells by Joseph Stieler (1781–1858), in 1817. Portrait of the Würzburg Lord Mayor and Privy Councillor Prof. Dr. Wilhelm Joseph Behr, painted in pastells by Johann Georg Hirschmann (1769–after 1820), in 1819. ● Writing-table made of cedar and rosewood with magnificent intarsia. A present of the city of Würzburg given on the occasion of the wedding of Crown-Prince Maximilian of Bavaria with Princess Marie of Prussia in 1842. Designed by the painter Andreas Geist (1805–1860), made by Johann Link (1819–1899) and Thomas Bauer (1809–1862) in the workshop of the master cabinet-maker Adam Barth (1815–1882).

*On the left-hand wall:* A portrait of Charlotte von Bechtolsheim as a child, painted in 1838 by Ferdinand von Rayski (1806–1890). By the same artist ● two large portraits of Philipp Freiherr von Bechtolsheim and Caroline Freifrau von Bechtolsheim with her son Moritz, both painted in Mainsondheim in 1838. Chest of drawers, South German, about 1830. Landscape painting of the ● Main River near Dettelbach by Ferdinand von Rayski, with a selfportrait of the painter, in 1837/38.

*On the end wall:* Grandfather clock with rotating pendulum, by the Würzburg watch and clockmaker Caspar Bollermann (1773–1829), about 1810. ● Portrait of Joseph Freiherr von Würtzburg painted by Ferdinand von Rayski in 1837. (On loan from the Federal Republic of Germany – a former possession of the German Reich). ● Portrait of Caroline Freifrau von Würtzburg, also painted by Ferdinand von Rayski, in 1837 (On loan from the Federal Republic of Germany – a former possession of the German Reich). Small sewing-table with rich intarsia, 1843, made by Adam Neppenbacher (1801–1848) after a design by Thomas Bauer. Large baroque clay stove with iron stokehole from Remlingen Palace, 1722.

*Portrait of Joseph Freiherr von Würtzburg, by Ferdinand von Rayski, 1837*

*On the right-hand wall:* Grandfather clock by the Bamberg watch and clockmaker Johann Georg Schmidt (1754–1830), about 1810. Pianoforte made by the Würzburg piano maker, Jacob Pfister (1770–1838), in 1808. ● Portrait of Josephine Freifrau Zobel von Giebelstadt zu Darstadt and a portrait of Edwin Freiherr Zobel von Giebelstadt zu Darstadt, painted by Ferdinand von Rayski, in 1838. By the same painter "Hunting Lodge in the Odenwald", with a self-portrait of the artist, about 1838.

*To the right of the entrance:* Oil painting "View of Würzburg from the Zeller Bock" by Andreas Geist (1805–1860), in 1844. ● Large oil painting "View of Würzburg from the Letzten Hieb" by Johann Georg Mauckner (1829–1862), in 1852. Chest of Drawers, probably Franconian, influenced by the workshop of David Roentgen, about 1790. Oil painting "View of Oberzell Cloister" by Andreas Geist, in 1844, and by August Christian Geist (1835–1868) "Harvest Day in the Franconian Alps", in 1860.

*Down the centre:* ● Sandstone figure "Removal of a Thorn" from the garden of the Veitshöchheim Castle, by Johann Peter Wagner (1730–1809), in 1771/72 (On loan from the Bayerische Verwaltung der Staatlichen Schlösser, Gärten und Seen).

*In the showcases:* Numerous pieces of work by the goldsmith Georg Stephan Dörffer (1771–1824), whose fame was widespread even during his lifetime, and of his successor Heinrich Riesing (died before 1846). Of special interest are the gold-plated silver sugar basin (belonging to a tea set), kept in the shape of a neo-classical covered goblet, two gold-plated salt receptacles made for the last Würzburg Prince-Bishop, Georg Karl von Fechenbach (1749–1808), two five-armed girandolas, as well as a large silver "tea-machine".

*View of Würzburg from the "Letzten Hieb"*
*by Georg Mauckner, 1852*

## To the left: Art Gallery (2)

The pictures shown here cover an impressive list of names,
such as Cornelis de Vos, Johann and Januarius Zick as well
as Giovanni Battista and Domenico Tiepolo, who were all
active at some time in Franconia. Here we see a rich diversity
of talents which only a collection belonging to a certain region
is able to present.

*Down the centre:* ● The groups of putti from the terrace of the former Prince-Bishops' summer residence in Veitshöchheim, by the court sculptor Johann Peter Wagner (1730–1809), in 1776/77, (On loan from the Bayerische Verwaltung der Staatlichen Schlösser, Gärten und Seen).

*1st partition on the right:* ● A group portrait of the Franconian family 'Hutten' by Cornelis de Vos (1585–1651), about 1625 (On loan from the Bayerische Staatsgemäldesammlungen Munich). *On the wall near the window:* Portrait of a girl (in 1681) by Johann Baptist Ruell (1634–1685), a Dutch artist who had moved to Würzburg. Chest of drawers, Franconian, about 1730. *On the left-hand wall:* Portrait of the Würzburg mayor, Nikolaus Ferdinand Schmitt, and his wife, painted in 1694 by an unknown Würzburg artist. A portrait in pastells of the Würzburg Prince-Bishop Johann Philipp von Greiffenclau (1652–1719), by Johann Matthäus Merian (1659–1716).

*1st partition on the left:* Portraits of the Würzburg Professor Jacob Amling and his wife painted by the Dutch artist Oswald Onghers (1628–1706), who had settled in Würzburg, painted about 1680. *On the outside wall:* Self-portrait of the Nuremberg painter, Johann Kupetzky (1667–1740), who also worked for the court in Würzburg, and his daughter, in 1713 (On loan from the Bayerische Staatsgemäldesammlungen Munich). A demiwardrobe with the coat of arms of the Cistercian Abbey Maria Bildhausen and of the Abbot Engelbert Klöpfel, Franconian, about 1735. *On the right-hand wall:* Works by the Swiss-born court painter Johann Rudolf Byss (1660–1738), who was commissioned for Pommersfelden Palace as well as for the Residence in Würzburg, "Feast of the Gods", in 1734, and "The Wedding Feast at Cana", in 1735, (On loan from the Bayerische Staatsgemäldesammlungen Munich). Grisaille painting in oil "A Tribute to the Prince Elector of Mainz and the Prince-Bishop of Bamberg Lothar Franz von Schönborn (1655–1729)", by Jacob Sandrart (1630–1708).

*Johann Peter Wagner, putto from Veitshöchheim, 1776/77*

*Marcus Friedrich Kleinert, portrait of Balthasar Neumann, 1727*

*2nd partition, on the right:* ● Portrait of the famous architect Balthasar Neumann (1687–1753), builder of the Residence and the churches at Vierzehnheiligen, Neresheim etc. by Marcus Friedrich Kleinert (1694–1742), in 1727. Further a portrait of Friedrich Karl von Schönborn (1674–1746), Prince-Bishop of Würzburg and Bamberg, builder of the Residence in Würzburg, by Johann Gottfried Auerbach (1697–1753), about 1730. *On the outer wall:* Large altar painting "Maria Immaculata and the Fourteen Merciful Saints" painted in 1732 for a Franconian cloister church by Joseph Anton Glantschnigg (1695–1755). *On the left-hand wall:* Design for an altar painting "Jesus Christ the Lord" for the Augustinian Church in Würzburg, in 1751/52, by Georg Anton Urlaub (1713–1759). By the same painter ● Self-portrait in pastells dating from the year 1735, as well as "The Glory of St. Bruno", design for a fresco for the former Carthusian monastery in Würzburg, about 1753/54. Exquisite small demiwardrobe, Würzburg, about 1750. *In the window recess:* Design for a (destroyed) ceiling fresco of the audience room of the Residence "Bishop Albert von Hohenlohe receives the fief of the Dukedom of Franconia from Emperor Karl IV", painted in 1735 by Johann Joseph Scheubel the Elder (1686–1769). Two Schönborn – allegories by Georg Anton Urlaub, about 1735.

*2nd partition, on the left:* Works of the famous Venetian Giovanni Battista Tiepolo (1696–1770) and his sons Domenico (1727–1804) and Lorenzo (1736–1776), partly dating from the time of their stay in Würzburg (1750–1753). "The Beheading of St. John the Baptist", coloured sketch for Tiepolo's fresco in Bergamo, about 1736. By Domenico Tiepolo ● two designs for the lintels in the Imperial Hall of the Residence "St. Ambrose and Emperor Theodosius" and "Emperor Constantine as the Defender of the Christian Faith", in 1751/52. Oil painting, head of a philosopher, by Lorenzo Tiepolo, in 1757. *On the outer wall:* "Anthony escorts Cleopatra to her ship", paint-

*Giovanni Battista Tiepolo, top: Design for the ceiling fresco*
*of the Imperial Hall of the Würzburg Residence, 1750/51*
*on the right: "Vocation of Cincinnatus", 1728/30*

ing by a Tiepolo-pupil modelled on Tiepolo's fresco in the
Palazzo Labia in Venice, about 1750.
Franconian commode with pewter and brass intarsia, about
1750/60. On the right-hand wall: "Vocation of Cincinnatus"
oil sketch by Giovanni Battista Tiepolo for the wall painting
in the Ca'Dolfin in Venice, about 1728/30, (On loan from
the Federal Republic of Germany – a former possession of
the German Reich). ● By the same painter, a first design for
the ceiling fresco of the Imperial Hall of the Würzburg Residence "Apollo leads Beatrix of Burgundy to her groom, Emperor Barbarossa", in 1751. From the atelier of Giovanni Battista Tiepolo, design for the fresco of the Villa Cordellina in
Montecchio Maggiore near Venice, about 1743.

26

*3rd partition, on the right:* Works by Johann Zick (1702–1762), who remained in Würzburg after being commissioned to decorate the Garden Hall of the Residence. Self-portrait of the artist and portrait of his wife, about 1750. A portrait of Franz Ludwig von Fichtel, who was chancellor to the Prince-Bishop in Würzburg. *On the outer wall:* ● Large oil sketch (1752) for the fresco of the staircase of Bruchsal Palace by Johann Zick. Commode, about 1740/50, probably by a Bamberg artist. *On the left-hand wall:* Portraits of the Würzburg court sculptor, Jacob von der Auvera and his wife, painted about 1751/53 by Lorenzo Tiepolo (1736–1776). Oil painting by Johann Zick, "The Good Samaritan", about 1750. *In the window-recess:* A further oil painting by Johann Zick, "St. Hieronymus", about 1750, and "The Glory of the Dominican Order" by Matthäus Günther (1705–1788), about 1740.

*3rd partition, on the left:* Three pictures by Januarius Zick (1730–1797), "Jesus Is Taken Down from the Cross", about 1760, "The Slaying of the Sabine King Titus Tatius", in 1752, and "The Sacrifice of Iphigenia", in 1752. "Adoration of the Shepherds" by Josepf Zoffany (1733–1810), painted about 1757, during the artist's stay in Würzburg. *On the outer wall:* ● A magnificent painting of the councillor, Franz Ludwig von Erthal (1730–1795), who was later to become the Prince-Bishop of Würzburg and Bamberg, painted in Rome in 1759 by Nikolaus Treu (1734–1786). Franconian commode, about 1730/40. *On the right-hand wall:* Oil paintings "Adoration of the Shepherds" and "Adoration of the Magi", painted in 1757 by Januarius Zick. ● By the same artist, a self-portrait in an intricately carved frame, about 1760. ● Beautiful woman's writing-table with magnificent intarsia, made by the Würzburg court cabinet-maker Johann Georg Fellweck, about 1775.

*Portrait of Franz Ludwig von Erthal, painted by Nikolaus Treu,*
*1759*

*4th partition, on the right:* Portrait of Adam Friedrich von Seinsheim (1708–1779), Prince-Bishop of Würzburg and Bamberg, painted in 1772 by Joseph Scheubel the Younger (1733–1801). Portrait of Johanna Nepomucena Knauer, prioress of the Dominican cloister in Bamberg, painted in 1754 by the painter Johann Anwander (1715–1770), who came from Donauwörth and worked for a time in Franconia. Portrait of Johann Baptist Broili, a Würzburg councillor and merchant, painted about 1750 by Georg Anton Urlaub (1713–1759). *On the outer wall:* Large portrait of Franz Schreiber, provost of the Augustinian canons' monastery in Heidenfeld on the Main River, painted in 1779 by Georg Karl Urlaub (1749–1811). Chest of drawers, probably by a Würzburg craftsman, about 1740/45. *On the left-hand wall:* Portrait of Octavian Salver, the Würzburg Prince-Bishop's archivist, and his wife, painted about 1765 by Georg Karl Urlaub (1749–1811). Self-portrait of Georg Anton Abraham Urlaub (1744–1788) together with Magdalena Uhl and Dorothea Uhl, about 1770. Small Franconian chest of drawers, about 1800. *In the window-recess:* Oil sketch "The Holy Trinity", by Andreas Urlaub (1735–1781), in 1769, and two pictures "St. Peter" and "St. Paul", painted about 1800 by the Weissenhorn painter Conrad Huber (1752–1830), who also worked in Würzburg.

*4th partition, on the left:* Two imaginary landscapes, by Christoph Treu (1739–1799). Portrait of Stephan Wolff, by Christoph Fesel (1737–1805). *On the outer wall:* Portrait of the last provost of the Augustinian canons' monastery in Heidenfeld, Mauritius Schmitt, painted in 1798 by Konrad Geiger. Commode with the coat of arms of the Cistercian Abbey Maria Bildhausen and of the abbot, Nivard Schlimbach, Franconian, about 1790. *On the right-hand wall:* Self-portrait of Carl Caspar Fesel (1775–1846). Further: "Landscape of the Main River near Miltenberg" by Christian Georg Schütz the Elder (1718–1791). Franconian commode, about 1790. ● Self-portrait of Margarethe Geiger (1783–1809), 1804.

*Würzburg artist, Mercy-seat, about 1340/50*

## The Gothic Gallery (3)

is devoted to Franconian sculpture from the 14th and 15th centuries, an era in which sculpture in Würzburg enjoyed its first great golden age. More sculpture in the Knights' Hall (12).

*On the right:* Virgin with Child, Würzburg, about 1400. ● Mercy-seat with donor, relief from the memorial chapel of the "Bürgerspital" bearing the Hospice's date of foundation in 1319, by a sculptor who was strongly influenced by the so-called "Master Wolfskeel", about 1340/50. Relief depicting the Annunciation, from the chapel of a former canonical residence (Rödelsee) in Würzburg, in 1484. *In the window-recess:* Franconian bust of a saint, about 1510, and Virgin with Child from Riemenschneider's workshop, about 1495/1500. Furthermore, a statue of the Enthroned Virgin with Child, Würzburg, about 1330. Another statue of the Blessed Virgin, from St. Stephen's Church in Bamberg, about 1360. And Virgin with Child, Würzburg, about 1370.

*On the left:* A sainted bishop, Würzburg, about 1370. Large, partially damaged statue of the Virgin with Child, Würzburg, about 1370. Two panel-paintings "Prophecy of St. Anne and St. Joachim" and "The Adoration of the Magi", by Friedrich Herlin (died 1499/1500), about 1490. Pietà from the cemetery chapel of St. Michael in Volkach, about 1410 by the so-called "Schwarzburg-Master". ● Alabaster Madonna taken from a Würzburg house – "Johanniterbäck" – made by an artist from the Central-Rhein River area, about 1360. Virgin with Child, Main-Franconian, about 1390.

## Riemenschneider Room (3)

"Master Til" was born in Heiligenstadt about 1460. He grew up in Osterode in the Harz Mountains. He came in 1483 to Würzburg after his years of travel as a journeyman and was granted citizenship here in 1485. The high esteem in which he was held in pulic life is borne out by his advancing from citizen to alderman and finally to mayor of the city. In 1525 he became involved in the destructive chaos of the Peasants' Revolt. Because he sided with the peasants' cause he was taken prisoner and tortured in the Randersacker Tower of the Fortress. He was released after eight weeks of imprisonment. Thereafter, with the exception of a few rare occasions, he was no longer active as an artist. He died on July 7th, 1531. His masterpieces, a large number of which are contained in this room, have now become as popular all over the world as they already were in Franconia during the artist's own lifetime.

*On the right:* St. Michael, Riemenschneider's workshop, about 1515. St. Anne, the Virgin and the Christ Child (Anna Selbdritt), from Grossostheim, Riemenschneider's workshop, about 1500. St. Catherine, Riemenschneider-school, about 1515/20. *On the outer wall:* Relief of St. Urban, Riemenschneider's workshop, about 1510. A sainted bishop, Franconian, about 1515. Two pietàs from Riemenschneider's-workshop and school, about 1510. St. Michael, Franconian, about 1515. Relief of St. Lawrence, from the former "Hospital for Incurables" located on the Steinberg in Würzburg, Riemenschneider's workshop, about 1510. *On the dividing-wall:* ● St. Nicholas, from the same hospital, by Tilman Riemenschneider, about 1510.

*On the left:* St. Nicholas, from the "Ehehaltenhaus" in Würzburg, Riemenschneider-school, about 1520/25. St. Anne, from a group of the Holy Family, from Lindelbach, Riemenschneider-school, about 1520/25. St. Barbara, Riemenschneider-school, about 1515/20.

*On the outer wall:* Panel-painting "St. Margaret", from Rothenburg o.d.T., by the Rothenburg painter, Martinus Schwarz, who had dealings with Riemenschneider (died about 1513), about 1500. Two sandstone figures-St. John the Baptist and St. Simon, taken from a depiction of all the apostles on the buttresses of the Marienkapelle (Chapel of the Virgin Mary) in Würzburg, by Tilman Riemenschneider, in 1500/06,

Panel-painting "St. Apollonia", from Rothenburg o.d.T. by Martinus Schwarz, about 1500. *On the partition:* ● St. Sebastian, by Tilman Riemenschneider, about 1515.

*Above the connecting doorway:* Crucifix from the church of the "Bürgerspital", by Tilman Riemenschneider, about 1515/20. *On the ceiling:* Twin Madonna by Tilman Riemenschneider from the Carmelite Church "St. Barbara" in Würzburg, about 1515/20.

*On the right:* ● Mourning Mary from a large Crucifixion group, which has been lost, exceptionally coloured, from Acholshausen, by Tilman Riemenschneider, about 1505. St. Hieronymus, Riemenschneider-school, about 1510. *On the pillar opposite:* ● St. Stephen by Tilman Riemenschneider, about 1520/25. *On the outer wall:* Relief of St. Dorothy, Riemenschneider-school, about 1500. ● St. Barbara from the "Ehehaltenhaus" in Würzburg, by Tilman Riemenschneider, about 1510. St. Kilian, from Burgebrach, by Tilman Riemenschneider, about 1510. St. John from a lost Crucifixion group, from the Rhön, by Tilman Riemenschneider, about 1505. ● Three sandstone statues of St. Paul, St. Judas Thaddeus, St. Matthew, from the row of apostles on the buttresses of the Marienkapelle (Chapel of the Virgin Mary) in Würzburg, by Tilman Riemenschneider, in 1500/06.

*On the left:* Virgin with Child, Riemenschneider's workshop, about 1520/25. St. James, Riemenschneider-school, about 1515/20. *On the pillar opposite:* St. Anne, the Virgin and the Christ Child (Anna Selbdritt), Tilman Riemenschneider, about 1500.

*On the outer wall:* Madonna, very weather-worn, from the Grabfeld, Riemenschneider's workshop, about 1510. ● Four statues of the apostles (sandstone): St. Thomas, St. Bartholomew, St. Philipp and St. James the Younger, from the row of apostles on the buttresses of the Marienkapelle (Chapel

*Tilman Riemenschneider, Virgin with Child (detail), about 1520*

of the Virgin Mary) in Würzburg, Tilman Riemenschneider, 1500/06.

*In a special showcase:* ● Small Madonna, limewood, Tilman Riemenschneider, about 1500. Mocking of Christ (Ecce-Homo devotional image), Riemenschneider's workshop, about 1515. Virgin Mary and St. John from a Crucifixion group, Riemenschneider's sphere of influence, about 1515/20. Two pietàs, made of paper pressed in moulds, Riemenschneider's sphere of influence, about 1520.

*On the end wall:* ● Adam and Eve; these two famous sandstone figures were sculpted by Tilman Riemenschneider in 1491/93 for the market portal of the Marienkapelle in Würzburg. *To the left of Adam:* Annunciation-group from the tabernacle above Adam, as well as the original pedestal for Adam, from the Marienkapelle located on the marketplace, by Tilman Riemenschneider, in 1493. Parts of a family-altar, exceptionally coloured, Riemenschneider's workshop, about 1505. *To the right of Eve:* Group-Christ and Magdalene from the tabernacle above Eve, as well as the original pedestal for Eve, from the Marienkapelle on the marketplace, by Tilman Riemenschneider, in 1493. Two reliefs "The Nativity" and "Adoration of the Magi" from the palace chapel in Aub, Riemenschneider's workshop, about 1510. Virgin with Child, Riemenschneider's sphere of influence, about 1515. *On the pillars* opposite Adam and Eve: ● Two angels with candlesticks, Tilman Riemenschneider, about 1502.

*On the far-end of the room:* Tilman Riemenschneider's tombstone from the former cathedral graveyard in Würzburg, by Jörg Riemenschneider, the artist's son, in 1531. ● Mary holding the Christ Child. This stone Madonna, which originally stood in the niche in the wall of the house of a cathedral dignitary in Würzburg, is a superb example of the late style of Riemenschneider, about 1520. It was moved abroad in the 19th century but brought back again in 1956. Two small crucifixes by Tilman Riemenschneider, about 1500 and 1505/10.

*Tilman Riemenschneider, angel with candlestick, about 1502*

## Showcase Corridor (4)

Unique collection of wood and clay models of the Franconian baroque and rococo eras. This collection stems mainly from the property of the last Würzburg court sculptor Johann Peter Wagner (1730–1809). Because of the great diversity of this collection, covering the whole range of 18th century Würzburg sculpture of artistic value, it is the leading collection of its kind.

*1st showcase on the left:* Clay models by the Würzburg court sculptor, Johann Wolfgang von der Auwera (1708–1756). ● St. Peter and St. Paul, intended for the high altar of the Cathedral in Worms, in 1741. St. John the Evangelist, meant for the pulpit of the Church of St. Peter in Würzburg, about 1750. Enthroned Mother of God with Child, for the pulpit in Burgwindheim, in 1753. Worshipping angel, for the high altar of the Franciscan church in Brühl, in 1745. ● Allegorical depiction of "Faith", intended for the epitaph of Lothar Franz von Schönborn, Prince-Elector of Mainz and Prince-Bishop of Bamberg (1655–1729), originally in the Cathedral in Bamberg, today located in the Schönborn Hall of the Mainfränkische Museum, about 1746. Minerva, Ceres and Urania for the statues along the revetment wall of the parterres of the Court Garden in Veitshöchheim, in 1752.

*1st showcase (right):* Franconian miniature sculpture of the rococo period. St. Sebastian, by the Würzburg sculptor, Daniel Köhler (1730–1778), about 1775. Model of an unknown Franconian rococo altar, about 1750. Virgin with Child, by the sculptor Johann Joseph Kessler (1711–1759), who came from Königshofen, about 1745/48. St. John Nepomuk, by the Neustadt artist Johann Caspar Hippeli (1716–1783), about 1760. "Baptism of the Negroes by St. Francis Xavier", by an unidentified sculptor, about 1740. Shrine with St. Sebastian, Franconian, about 1750.

*2nd showcase (right):* Charlemagne, model for the statue on the Old Main Bridge in Würzburg, by the Würzburg court

*Johann Peter Wagner, clay models for the 1st station
of the Via Crucis (Stations of the Cross)
leading up to the Käppele, about 1775*

sculptor Claude Curé (1685–1745), in 1730/32. Base of an obe-
lisk of the former gate of honour in front of the Residence
in Würzburg, by Johann Wolfgang von der Auwera, in 1741.
St. John Nepomuk, model for the statue on the Old Main
Bridge in Würzburg, by Johann Sebastian or Volkmar Becker
from Hassfurt, about 1725. Angel with cornucopia, by Johann
Wolfgang von der Auwera, about 1740.
*2nd showcase (left):* ● Clay models for the famous Via Crucis
leading up to the Käppele in Würzburg, by Johann Peter
Wagner, 1767–1778.
*3rd showcase (left):* Models for ecclesiastical equipment, altar
figures and architectural sculpture etc. by Johann Peter

Wagner. Angel with escutcheon, about 1765/70. St. Clement, for the high altar of the Trimberg church, 1772. St. Anne, for the high altar of the pilgrimage-church "Maria Limbach", in 1760/61. St. Sebastian, for the "Sebastian's Column" in Eibelstadt, in 1773. St. Nicholas, for a side-altar in Wettringen, in 1786. Virgin with Child, after the model of the Mannheim court sculptor Paul Egell (1691–1752), about 1755/60. St. Peter and an unfinished variation of the same figure, as well as the ● large groups depicting the glorification of St. Benedict and St. Bernard, for the high altar in Ebrach, in 1779. The Flagellation of Christ, 1770/75. Maria Immaculata, modelled after a figure by Paul Egell, about 1755/60. Anatomist, for the old Institute of Anatomy of the Würzburg "Juliusspital"-Hospital, 1788/89. St. Thomas, for a side-altar in Ebrach, in 1782/85. St. Wendelin, for a side-altar in Grafenrheinfeld, in 1766/67. St. John, from the altar in Grafenrheinfeld, 1778/79. Warrior, about 1775. Two allegorical figures by Balthasar Heinrich Nickel (1743–1799), a pupil of Johann Peter Wagner, about 1795.

*3rd showcase (right):* Miniature sculpture by the Würzburg wood-carver Johann Benedict Witz (1709–1780), whose main occupation was soldiering. Attendant-figures of Crucifixion group, 1756. St. Aquiline, after 1775. The Death of St. Francis Xavier, about 1775/80. Lamentation of the Blessed Virgin, about 1765. Lamentation of Christ, about 1765. Adoration of the Magi, about 1745/50. Maria Immaculata with Adam and Eve, about 1770/75. Adoration of the Shepherds, about 1770/80. Christ as the Good Shepherd and Mary as Help of Sinners, about 1760/62. The Holy Family, about 1765. Adoration of the Shepherds, about 1780. Self-portrait of Johann Benedict Witz on the back of a reliquary, about 1762/65 (On loan from the Deutschordenmuseum Bad Mergentheim). Head of St. Joseph which originally also had a small plaque mounted in it, from a processional statue in Münnerstadt, in 1749. Base of a Crucifix, 1774.

*Last showcase:* Clay models for figures meant for gardens, among other things, by Johann Peter Wagner. Mars and Franconia, for the Garden of the Würzburg Residence, about 1775/80. Neptune, for the cascade in the Garden of the Summer Residence in Veitshöchheim, in 1772/73. Fountain-group and Neptune, about 1772/73. The figures of Summer and Winter, for the Staircase of the Residence in Würzburg, about 1773. ● Diana, for the figure of "Bathing Diana" for the cascade in the Court Garden in Veitshöchheim, in 1772/73. Ceres, for the same Garden. ● The figure "Removal of a Thorn", meant for the figure which originally stood in the Court Garden at Veitshöchheim, but is now in the "Stein" Room of the Mainfränkische Museum (1 a), in 1771/72. Zephyr and Flora, about 1770. Group of putti, for the Staircase of the Würzburg Residence, in 1773. Young man sitting down, about 1775/80.

*Other exhibits in the room:* Commode with additional cupboard on top, Würzburg, about 1745. ● Flaggelation of Christ, alabaster statue by Johann Peter Wagner, in 1779. Further, an alabaster relief "The Communion of St. Mary Magdalene", by Johann Peter Wagner, about 1780/85, and by the same artist a relief in clay "Meeting of the hermits St. Anthony and St. Paul", about 1780. In a table-showcase reliefs by Johann Benedict Witz. "Cain and Abel", about 1775/80. St. Hieronymus and St. Mary Magdalene, about 1770/75. "St. Joseph's Dream", about 1765. "Madonna in Protecting Cloak" and "Jesus Christ the Good Shepherd", about 1770. House organ in beautiful cabinet, by David Jacob Weidner, Augsburg, 1700, from Schwanberg Castle in the Steigerwald. Designs for two unknown high altars, by the sculptor Johann Caspar Hippeli from Neustadt (1716–1783), about 1765. Figure of Mary with Child and angels, by Balthasar Esterbauer (1672–1728). Water-colour depicting the last Würzburg court sculptor, Johann Peter Wagner (1730–1809) surrounded by his family, by Martin Wagner (1777–1858).

## Views of the City (5)

This collection comprises numerous views of Würzburg from 1493 to 1945 and shows the development of the city from late medieval times to the fire which destroyed the city.

*1st partition left:* Mirror from the Butchers' Guild Room, in 1738. ● Bird's-eye view of Würzburg, copper-plate engraving made F.W. von Reitzenstein, after a drawing by Balthasar Neumann (1687–1753), engraved by Johann Salver (1673–1738), in 1723. Iron chest, masterpiece of the Würzburg locksmith, Marcus Gattinger (1713–1753), in 1742. Punch-press from the chancelry of the chapter house of the Cathedral in Würzburg, by the Würzburg court locksmith, Johann Georg Oegg (1703–1782), in 1748. View of Würzburg from the east, coloured etching by Franz Hogenberg (before 1540–1590), from Georg Braun's: "Civitates orbis terrarum", Cologne in 1572. ● View of Würzburg from the east, coloured woodcut from the "Book of Chronicles" by Hartmann Schedel, Nuremberg in 1493. Würzburg from the east, coloured woodcut by Hans Rudolph Manuel Deutsch (1525–1570), from Sebastian Münster's Cosmography, Basel in 1548. *In the special case:* Glass goblet with lid bearing the coat of arms of the Würzburg Prince-Bishop Johann Gottfried von Guttenberg (1645–1698) and a view of the Fortress Marienberg, by Heinrich Schwanhardt, Nuremberg about 1685. Tip of a Würzburg flag-pole with the coat of arms of Prince-Bishop Johann Philipp von Schönborn (1605–1673) and a portrayal of Patrona Franconiae (Patroness of Franconia), 1660. Medal commemorating the good harvest in the year 1706, by Georg Hautsch (1664–1736), Nuremberg, 1706, and a medal of Johann Philipp von Schönborn as Prince-Bishop of Würzburg, between 1642 and 1647. Processional figures of Maria Immaculata and St. Joseph, from Nüdlingen in the Rhön, by the sculptor, Johann Joseph Kessler from Königshofen (1711–1759), about 1750. ● Magnificent twin cupboard from the vestry of the Premonstratensian Ab-

*Dedicatory page of the serial issue of the "Flight to Egypt",
by Giovanni Domenico Tiepolo, 1753*

bey in Oberzell near Würzburg, the cabinet-making work was
done by the Würzburg court cabinet-maker Carl Maximilian
Mattern (1704–1774), the ornate wood-carvings are from the
court sculptor Johann Wolfgang von der Auwera (1708–1756).
*1st partition right:* Heraldic calender of the Würzburg Cathedral chapter, copper engraving by Johann Balthasar Gutwein
(1702–1785), after a drawing by Anton Joseph Högler
(1707–1786), in 1768. Clay stove from Willanzheim, dating
from about 1670, with cast-iron stokehole, in 1599. Christ
Child giving His blessing, by Lucas von der Auvera
(1710–1766), about 1755. Three copperplate engravings by Johann Leipold, "The Old University", "Juliusspital" and
"Marienberg Castle", in 1604. *In the special showcase:* Among

other things: A gold-plated silver confectionery-bowl belonging to the Würzburg Prince-Bishop Julius Echter von Mespelbrunn (15454–1617), about 1590. Four books from the library of Prince-Bishop Julius Echter with the "supralibros" of the ruler on the embossed pigskin book-covers, by the Würzburg book-binder, Georg Freyberger.

*2nd partition left:* Würzburg in the year 1632, copperplate engraving by Matthäus Merian (1593–1650), from the "Topographia Franconiae", Frankfurt in 1648. From the same work – "Fortress Marienberg and the Old Main Bridge in Würzburg". View of the Fortress Marienberg from the south-west, etching by Mathäus Merian after Wenzel Hollar (1607–1677), in 1648. Bird's-eye view of Würzburg, coloured etching out of the "Atlas" by Johann Baptist Homann (1664–1724), Nuremberg in 1723. The Old Main Bridge seen from the south and from the north, two etchings by Wolfgang Högler (1674–1754), in 1727. View of Würzburg from the north, coloured etching by Salomon Kleiner (1703–1761), in 1725. *In the table-showcase:* Seals and signet-rings from the city of Würzburg as well as from its guilds. Further, keys of the city of Würzburg, early 19th century.

*2nd partition right:* Ten pictures of Würzburg during the baroque era, etchings by Salomon Kleiner, 1725. *In the table-showcase:* Medals and medallions of the Würzburg Prince-Bishops in the 18th century. ● Further – mock fossils, the so-called "Lügensteine" (lying/deceiving stones) and the book "Lithographiae Wirceburgensis" by Johann Bartholomäus Beringer in which the discovery of these stones is mentioned, in 1726.

*3rd partition left:* ● Dedicatory page of the serial issue (etchings) "Flight to Egypt" with a view of the Fortress, by Domenico Tiepolo (1727–1804), in 1753. From the same serial issue "The Holy Family Approaching a Town"; in the background, the Marienberg Fortress with the "Maschikuli-Tower", 1753. Bird's-eye view of the Würzburg Residence, copperplate en-

*Würzburg porcelain, 1775/80*

graving by Johann Balthasar Gutwein (1702–1785) after a drawing by Michael Anton Müller (1693–1772), about 1770. The Court Church ("Hofkirche") of the Würzburg Residence, etching by Johann Balthasar Gutwein after a drawing by Balthasar Neumann (1687–1753), in 1744. Würzburg – viewed from the north, gouache painting by Peter Sprenger, about 1790. View of Würzburg from the south-west, lithography by Gustav Kraus (1804–1852), in 1828. View of Würzburg from the north, coloured etching by Johann Adam Klein (1792–1875), in 1811. *In the showcase:* ● Some examples of the articles produced by the rather short-lived (1775 to 1780) Würzburg Porcelain Manufactory of the Councillor of the Consistory and Privy Chancery Clerk, Johann Caspar Geyger. *In the table-showcase:* Among other objects-keys belonging to the Würzburg chamberlains, made by the Würzburg court locksmith, Johann Georg Oegg (1703–1782) and ● measuring instrument belonging to Balthasar Neumann (1687–1753), a so-called proportional compass, used for figuring out the different orders of columniation, in 1713.

*3rd partition right:* Two lithographies by Fritz Bamberger (1814–1873) – "Parade at the District Agricultural Fair in front of the Würzburg Residence" and "Fishermen's mock-fight held on the river in Würzburg", 1842. Würzburg from the south-west, coloured contour-etching by Christian Friedrich August Richter (1781/82–1854) and Christian Gottlob Hammer (1779–1864), in 1818. ● Oil painting "Marienkapelle and Market-Place in Würzburg with a rich array of traditional costumes", by Peter Geist (1816–1867), about 1845. Two lithographies by Friedrich Kaiser (1815–1890), "A Sunday Morning in the Würzburg Court Gardens" and "Arrival of the Steamboat 'Leopold' on the Main River in Würzburg", about 1845. Würzburg with a view from the Zell country road, steelplate engraving by Ludwig Richter (1803–1884), in 1837. Würzburg from the north and from the east, two coloured lithographies by Gustav Frank, about 1860. *In the special showcase:* Porcelain dating from the first half of the 19th century with different views of Würzburg, for example-works of Christian Friedrich Carl Thomin, a porcelain painter who worked in Würzburg from 1807 to 1812. *In the table-showcase:* Würzburg in the 19th century.

*4th partition left:* "Town Hall with Four-Pipe Fountain" and "The Old Crane, the Old Main Bridge and the Fortress Marienberg", two pencil drawings by William Henry Harriot, in 1830. Würzburg with a view from the Steinberg, watercolour by Joseph Andreas Weiss (1814–1887), in 1883. "Würzburg on March 16th, 1945", watercolour by Fried Heuler (1889–1959), in 1945. ● View of the "Kürschnerhof" (furrier's courtyard) in Würzburg, large watercolour by William Callow (1812–1908), in 1848. *In a table-showcase:* Coffee-set for two persons, with numerous views of Würzburg, from the Royal Prussian Porcelain Manufactory in Berlin, about 1895.

*4th partition right:* Numerous watercolour paintings with motifs taken from the Würzburg of former times, by the English artist, Samuel Prout (1783–1852), about 1825, and often used as models from which lithographies were copied. "The Herrengasse with the Conti Palace". "The Tivoli Pavilion". Two imaginary scenes using Würzburg motifs. "The Old Main Bridge and the Fortress Marienberg". The accompanying lithographies are to be found in the table-showcase. ● View of the upper Market-place with the Marienkapelle and the Falkenhaus (House of the Falcon), large watercolour painting by Samuel Prout, about 1825. Further – a coin-box, once belonging to Carl Friedrich Wilhelm von Erthal, Canon of the Cathedral, made by the Bamberg court joiner Balthasar Hermann (about 1744–1778), in 1778.

*Samuel Prout, View of the Upper Market-Place with Marienkapelle and Falkenhaus, about 1825*

47

*On the end walls:* ● Portable gilded decorative carvings, probably originally located in the Würzburg Residence, by Johann Wolfgang von der Auwera (1708–1756), about 1745/50. ● By the same sculptor, two mourning angels – all that is left of the baroque decor and furnishings of the altar in the Würzburg Marienkapelle, in 1753.

*Down the centre:* Six 18th century Franconian processional poles. Four richly carved wooden ledges from confessionals in the Church of St. Augustine in Würzburg, from the workshop of Johann Wolfgang von der Auwera, about 1750/55. ● Splendid wrought-iron chandelier from the parish of Allersheim, which belonged to the former Cistercian monastery in Bronnbach, made by Wolf Krebs (about 1590 – before 1642), in 1617.

## Faïence Room (6)

The years of splendour of the baroque and rococo periods in Franconia are shown in the following rooms, with fine furniture from palaces, abbeys and patrician houses, with sculptures, painting and ceramics etc. The colourful variety of the faïences of southern and central German manufacture is revealed in the showcases.

*1st. showcase on the right:* Products of the faïence manufacturies of Frankfurt on Main (1666–1772) and Hanau (1661–1806). Below, includes Hanau mugs with coats of arms of a number of Prince Bishops of Würzburg as well as some items from the faïence manufacturies of Heusenstamm (1662–1666) and Offenbach (1759–after 1807).

*1st. showcase on the left:* Products of the Ansbach faïence manufactury (1709–1804). Above: ● magnificent items with "cold decor" ornamentation.

*2nd. showcase on the right:* Products from the faïence manufactures of Crailsheim (about 1720–1827), Wiesbaden (1770–1795), Flörsheim (1765–1922), Künersberg

(1745–1767/68), Mosbach (1770–1828), Durlach (1723–1840) and Göggingen (1748–1752).

*2nd. showcase on the left:* Above: Products of the Bayreuth faïence manufactury (1714–1835), including brown-ware with gold ornamentation and a clock case with silver ornamentation painted by the faïence painter, Johann Abraham Fichthorn. Centre: Products of the Nuremberg faïence manufactury (1712–1840). Below: Products of the Fulda faïence manufactury (1741–1758), including three figures from a series of seasons. Items from the faïence manufactures of Öttingen-Schrattenhofen (1735–1745 and 1757 to about 1830), Schrezheim (1732–1752), Friedberg (1754–1768), Ludwigsburg (1758–1824), Brunswick (1710–1807) and Dorotheenthal (about 1707/08)–1803 or 1806).

*Left:* Wardrobe, Franconian, about 1750, used as a display cabinet with a magnificent ● collection of Ansbach faïences of the so-called "Green Family". These copies of Chinese porcelain of the K'ang-Hsi period (1662–1722) are masterpieces of German faïence art. The mastery and the secret lie not in the colour but in the flux with which the colours were applied and fired.

*Right:* Wardrobe, southern German. 1st third of the 18th century; used as a cabinet with an excellent ● collection of various faïences of Nuremberg and Bayreuth manufactury, painted by Georg Friedrich Grebner. Wardrobe, Würzburg, about 1740/50; used as a cabinet, with a very fine ● collection of what were known as home-painted faïences. Soon after the foundation of the first German faïence manufactury, "home painters" appeared as independent specialists, and they decorated unpainted articles in their own homes. It is their colourfulness and their variety which make them so distinctive. Magnificent items by the Nuremberg Home painters Wolfgang Rößler (1655–1717), Justus Alexander Ernst Glüer, Abraham Helmhack (1654–1724), by Bartholomäus Seuter of Augsburg

(1678–1754) and of Joseph Philipp Dannhöfer who worked in Fulda and Bayreuth.

*On the walls:* Supraporte above the entrance. Portrait of the Privy Councillor of the Würzburg Prince-Bishop and General Hugo Gottfried von Eisenberg and his wife by Anton Spahn (1724–after 1779), about 1750. Astronomical clock with an engraved map of the world, by Johann Balthasar Gutwein (1702–1785), the case by the Würzburg court cabinetmaker, Carl Maximilian Mattern (1704–1774), about 1743. Wardrobe with rich marquetry, by the court cabinetmaker from Wiesentheid, Johann Georg Neßtfell (1694–1762), about 1730. On top of the wardrobe, a set of vases of Ansbach faïence. ● Bureau of Baron Ferdinand Christoph Peter von Sickingen, Privy Councillor of the Prince-Bishop of Würzburg and District President, made by the Würzburg court cabinetmaker, Servatius Arend (1673–1729), 1729. ● Two richly carved panels with mirrors from the audience chamber in the Prince-Bishop's former summer palace "Seehof" near Bamberg, 1751/52, created by Bonaventura Joseph Mutschele (1728–1778 or 1783) and Nikolaus Bauer (about 1699–1771). Console table, Franconian, about 1770. On top, table-fountain of faïence with "cold" decor, perhaps from the Schrezheim manufacture about 1770. Double wardrobe, Franconian, 1st half of 17th century. Herm bust "Forest nymph Silva", from the garden of the summer palace at Veitshöchheim, by Ferdinand Tietz, 1767. Supraporte above the door, hunting portrait of Charlotte von Thüngen, by Franz Anton Spahn (1724–after 1779) about 1750. Herm bust "Summer" from the court garden in Veitshöchheim, by Ferdinand Tietz, 1767. ● Large tiered facade cupboard from Ebrach Abbey, masterpiece by a cabinetmaker from Augsburg, about 1680. Large faïence bowl from Bayreuth, 2nd third of 18th century, set into a washstand in the 19th century. Nightstool in the form of two leather-bound folios, from a Franconian palace, about 1790. Large floor vase from the Ansbach faïence manufacture, 2nd third of 18th cen-

*Nuremberg faïence "home-painted" jugs, 1680/1725*

tury. Bureau of the Würzburg Prince Bishop, Johann Philipp von Greiffenclau (1652–1719), made about 1713 by the Würzburg court cabinetmaker, Servatius Arend and decorated with gilded copper plates from the commemorative publication, "Gryphus Principalis" by Johann Valentin Kirchgeßner. In the window recess a 1956 copy of the copper plate from the middle part of the bureau for the frontespiece "Coelus Herbipolense", engraved in 1712 by Johann Salver (1673–1738). Large floor vase from the Ansbach faïence manufacture, 2nd third of 18th century. Nightstool from the Keerl house in Marktsteft, made in 1788 on the occasion of a visit by the Margrave Alexander von Brandenburg-Ansbach. Cabinet from Pommersfelden palace, Franconian master, about 1720.

Limewood figure Maria Immaculata, by Georg Reuß (1704–1768), about 1745.

*In the centre of the room:* Twelve chairs covered with canework from Fulda, about 1740. On the walls around the room numerous faïences from various south German manufactures.

## Garden Room (7)

The original figures by the Würzburg and Bamberg court sculptor, Ferdinand Tietz, (1708–1777) from the garden of the Prince-Bishops' former summer palace at Veitshöchheim near Würzburg are exhibited here (on loan from the Bayerische Verwaltung der Staatlichen Schlösser, Gärten und Seen). They were made between 1765 and 1768. These spirited, light-hearted sandstone figures are a delightful treasure of Franconian rococo. In the garden where they stood originally, they have been replaced by copies.

*On either side of the entrance:* Dancing couple. Two large allegorical groups of ● spring and summer.

*Left*: Personification of the four continents known at the time, Europe, America, Africa and Asia. Statue of the god of war, Mars.

*On either side of the exit:* Allegorical group representing winter. ● A gentleman and lady playing musical instruments. Figures of Neptune and Chronos.

*Right*: Figure of Venus. Two groups showing the fox and the stork from Aesop's fables. Above, coat of arms of the Würzburg Prince-Bishop, Johann Philipp von Greiffenclau (1652–1719) as well as the Würzburg and Bamberg Prince-Bishop, Friedrich Karl von Schönborn (1674–1746).

*In the centre of the room:* ● Statue of the messenger of the gods, Mercury.

*Ferdinand Tietz,*
*Dancer from*
*Veitshöchheim*
*Palace Garden,*
*about 1767/68*

53

*On the pillars:* Four putti dancing a minuet. Also busts on Herm pilasters.

*In the showcase on the left:* Model figures by Ferdinand Tietz for statues in the garden of the former Prince-Bishops' summer palace "Seehof" near Bamberg. ● Large, gilded group, "Rape of Porsepina", 1748. Also hunting group, stag, a moor on a fountain basin as well as a bozzetto for a statue of Flora.

*In the showcase on the right:* Models by Ferdinand Tietz. Dancer with putto. Sphinx with putto. Personifications of Europe, Asia and Africa, from the Würzburg Cabinetmakers' Guild chest. Bozzetti for the allegorical presentation of Evening and Night from the Court Garden in Veitshöchheim, now in the entrance hall of the Mainfränkische Museum, 1766/67. Bozzetto for the statue of the Cavalier playing music, 1767/68, near the exit. St. Sebastian for the facade of the church in Gerlachsheim, about 1740. A bozzetto charred in the town fire of 1945 for a putto and a cherub from an altar.

## Rococo Room (8)

Fine rococo suite with original covers, from a palace in the Rhön area, about 1750.

*On the wall on the left:* Console table with elaborate carving, Bayreuth, about 1750. Above it, a magnificent mirror, southern German, about 1750. Two small, gilded console tables by Johann Joseph Keßler (1711–1759), probably from the Abbey of Maria Bildhausen, about 1755. Two cherubs in original mounting, by Ignaz Günther (1725–1775), about 1765. Two cherubs, southern German, about 1760. Portrait of the Empress Maria Theresia (1717–1780) and the Emperor Franz Stephan (1708–1765) by Philippe Joseph Tassaert (1732–1803), about 1760.

*On the window side:* ● Portrait in an elaborate gold frame of Theresia, Countess of Seinsheim, married Countess of Preysing, by Georg Desmarées (1697–1776), 1762.

*On the right:* ● Portrait of the Prince-Bishop of Würzburg, Carl Philipp von Greiffenclau (1690–1754), by Franz Anton Ermeltraut (1717–1767), in a magnificent rococo frame by the court sculptor of Würzburg, Johann Wolfgang von der Auvera (1706–1756), 1749. ● Ornate grandfather clock, case by the Würzburg court cabinetmaker, Carl Maximilian Mattern (1704–1774), carving by Johann Wolfgang von der Auvera, about 1743. ● Music desk of the Prince-Bishop of Würzburg and Bamberg, Friedrich Karl von Schönborn (1674–1746), by the Wiesentheid cabinetmaker, Johann Georg Neßtfell (1694–1762), about 1730/35.

*On either side of the little door:* Two pilaster herms by Johann Baptist Straub (1704–1784), about 1750. By the same artist: the cherub above the door, about 1760.

*Above the main doors:* Supraporte with portaits of Maria Magdalena von Erthal and Maria Anna von Erthal, painted by Franz Anton Spahn (1724–after 1779), about 1750. Supraporte with portaits of Elisabeth von Quad, née von Thüngen and Sophie von Tettenborn, painted by Franz Anton Spahn, about 1750.


**Tapestry Room (9)**

Painted fabric wall-covering from Schernau Palace near Kitzingen of landscape with figures, about 1725, painted by Zacharias König in Dettelbach. Parquet flooring from the baroque era, from a house in Würzburg.

*On the left:* cast iron stove made in the foundry of the Electorate of Mainz in Lohr, from Remlingen Palace about 1725.

Franconian console table, about 1740. ● Table clock with chiming mechanism, made by the Bamberg court clockmaker, Leopold Hoys (1713–1797), about 1750. Two violins, Augsburg, about 1700.

*On the window side:* Small side-table, Franconian, about 1750. Faïence statuette of St. John Nepomuk from the Schrezheim manufacture, by Martin Mutschele (1733–1804), about 1770. Small faïence charcoal stove, about 1750, birdcage, from Rothenburg ob der Tauber.

*On the right:* ● Magnificent bureau with rich ivory inlay, made in 1745 for the Prince-Bishop of Würzburg and Bamberg, Friedrich Karl von Schönborn (1674–1746), by the court cabinetmaker in Würzburg, Carl Maximilian Mattern (1704–1774) and decorated with carving by the court sculptor, Johann Wolfgang von der Auwera (1708–1756). After its rejection by the Prince-Bishop, the coat of arms was altered for Schönborn's successor, Anselm Franz von Ingelheim (1683–1749). Armchair with footstool, Franconian, about 1750.

### Ante-chamber (10)

*On the left:* Portrait of the Imperial Field Marshall, Hermann Christoph von Rußwurm, by an unknown artist, about 1630. Chest with inlay work, Franconian, 2nd half 16th century. Above: ● large silk tapestry from the former Ladies' Institution of Waizenbach in the Sinn valley; in the centre, coats of arms and the date 1688, on the older border from the second third of the 16th century, the coats of arms of Franconian families. Portrait of the Prince-Bishop of Würzburg, Friedrich von Wirsberg (1504–1573), by an unknown Würzburg artist. In front ● lectern belonging to the same regent, 1573, with alabaster reliefs, on the lid of the lectern, coats of arms of

*Carl Maximilian Mattern, bureau, 1745*

the Prince-Bishop, the Cathedral Chapter and the Duchy of Franconia.

*On the window side:* Sketch for a glass painting with the coat of arms of Prince-Bishop Friedrich von Wirsberg, 1573. Large portrait of Jacob Bauer von Eiseneck, Colonel of the Würzburg and Bamberg Catholic League troops at the beginning of the Thirty Years' War, by an unknown artist, about 1620.

*On the end wall:* Portrait of Johann Christoph Neustetter, known as Stürmer (Stormer), Imperial Councillor and Canon of Würzburg, Bamberg and Mainz, painted in 1635 by Matthäus Pinnet. Small iron chest, 17th century. Above the doorway to the Knights' Hall in its original position, tympanum with the coat of arms of the Würzburg Prince-Bishop, Johann Philipp von Greiffenclau (1652–1719), builder of the baroque arsenal, probably by Balthasar Esterbauer (1672–1728), about 1712. Chest with rich inlay work, Franconian, about 1600. Portrait of the Würzburg Prince-Bishop Julius Echter von Mespelbrunn (1545–1617), in the background the old Juliusspital in Würzburg, painted by an unknown Würzburg master, end 16th century.

*On the right:* Wall tile with the ducal and Bavarian coat of arms, by Hans Kraut (1532–1592), 2nd third of 16th century. Lavoir of potter's ceramic, Nuremberg, about 1550.

## Gothic Chamber (11)

*On the left:* Panel painting "St. Martin", Franconian, about 1510. Stool from Brendlorenzen/Saale, 17th century. Large wooden chest with iron bands, Franconian, 15th century. Wooden panel painting "The Resurrection of Christ", probably by Michael Wohlgemut (1434–1519), about 1490.

*Mechanical clock, southern German, about 1350*

*On the window side:* Oldest known ● mechanical clock, so-called "watchman's clock", south German, about 1350. Group of carved figures, "The Feast at Simon's" with Christ and Mary Magdalene, Franconian, about 1510 (on loan from the Federal Republic of Germany from former German Reich possessions). Wooden alms chest, Würzburg, 1538. Folding stool, south German, 16th century. Early gothic double window from the former "Deutscher Hof" in Würzburg, about 1250.

*On the right:* Late gothic writing desk, south German, about 1530. Pewter jug from Gerolzhofen, Nuremberg master, beginning of 16th century. Two small cabinet cupboards with inlay work, 16th century. Sandstone relief: "Virgin and Child", from a Würzburg building, unknown Würzburg master, about 1530. Arched door with iron mountings, Franconian, about 1450. Wooden panel painting "Maria Salome and St. Elizabeth", south German about 1480 (on loan from the Federal Republic of Germany from former German Reich possessions).

*On the floor:* Gothic tiles.

*On the ceiling:* ● Chandelier with the coat of arms of the town of Ochsenfurt, from the town hall in Ochsenfurt, by Tilman Riemenschneider (about 1460–1531) about 1510/15.
The stairs down to the *Echter bastion,* built by the Nuremberg architect, Jacob Wolff the Elder (about 1546–1612) in 1605, under Prince-Bishop Julius Echter von Mespelbrunn (1545–1617) as western bulwark for the Marienberg Fortress.

# Knights' Chamber (12)

The room is dominated by the sombre gothic and the ornate renaissance tombs. This is where the popular museum concerts are held every year during Advent.

*On the left:* Sandstone relief of St. John the Baptist, from the former St. John's commendam in Würzburg, 1330. Tombstone from the mediaeval Würzburg Jewish cemetry, 1347. Limewood relief "Fourteen Merciful Saints", from the Church of the Würzburg Hofspital, Riemenschneider workshop, perhaps Jörg Riemenschneider, about 1520/1530. Chest from the town poor house "Zum Gabler", near St. Peter's in Würzburg, 1535. Votive picture of the Lorber family with the Holy Trinity, after an engraving by Albrecht Dürer (1471–1528), Franconian artist, 1580 (lent by Bayerische Nationalmuseum in Munich). ● Anna Selbdritt, sandstone figure from Kitzingen, Tilman Riemenschneider (about 1460–1531), about 1495. Votive picture of Katharina Zolner, Franconian master, about 1520 (lent by the Bayerische Nationalmuseum in Munich). Limewood bust of a young saint, Franconian-Swabian master, about 1500 (lent by the Federal Republic of Germany from former German Reich possessions). Wrought iron tabernacle door with coat of arms of the Würzburg Prince-Bishop, Julius Echter von Mespelbrunn (1545–1617), 1603.

*Opposite the entrance:* ● Multi-figured alabaster tombstone of Valentin Echter von Mespelbrunn, the brother of Prince-Bishop Julius, with his family, by Julius Emes of Gaibach 1614/15. Sandstone relief with Valentin and Ottilia Echter von Mespelbrunn, the founders of the old parish church in Gaibach, 1588. Two kings from an adoration group, from the parish church in Gerolzhofen, Franconian master, about 1520. ● "The Death of the Virgin", in a coloured relief, from the hospital church in Gerolzhofen, from the school of the Nuremberg master, Veit Stoß (before 1450–1553), about 1490.

*On the wall on the right:* tombstone of Eberhard von Wolfs-keel, from Heiligenthal Abbey, about 1379. Tombstone of Margret Smidein of Würzburg, about 1456. Above: death shield of a member of the Hübner family of Nuremberg, 1462 (lent by the Germanische Nationalmuseum in Nuremberg). ● Tombstone of Friedrich von Wolfskeel from Heiligenthal Ab-bey, from the workshop of the so-called "Schwarzburg mas-ter", 1408. Tombstone of Johann Joseph Lang, bailiff of the Würzburg Teutonic Knights' commendam in Würzburg, 1750. Tombstone of Christoph von Köln, from the Würzburg Hof-spital, by Peter Dell the Younger (about 1520/25–1572), 1564. Tombstone of the master tailor, Peter Streck, from Burgsinn, 1625. Tombstone of Wolf Albert Echter von Mespelbrunn, by Zacharias Juncker (about 1578/80 – about 1657), from Gai-bach, 1636. ● Tombstone of Eberhard von Ehingen, com-mander of the Teutonic Knights' Commendam in Würzburg, from the Deutschhauskirche, by Peter Dell the Younger, about 1550 (lent by the Bayerische Nationalmuseum in Munich). Tombstone of Maria Justina Echter von Mespelbrunn, from Gaibach, by Zacharias Juncker, 1627.

*On the right:* ● Stone coat of arms of Pankraz von Redwitz from Tannenberg Court in Paradeplatz, Würzburg, Rie-menschneider workshop, 1498. Chest, south German, 15th cen-tury. Sandstone figure, Mourning Virgin, Würzburg, about 1350. ● Figures on the Mount of Olives from the former Ritter-stift of St. Burkard in Würzburg, by Tilman Riemenschneider, 1511. Sandstone figure Virgin and Child, Würzburg, about 1300. Relief from the Tomb of Countess Kunigunde Hojos, step-daughter of Count Konrad zu Castell, made by Peter Dell the Younger from the old parish church of Castell, 1572.

Four bronze candelabra, 17th century. The fine baroque lat-

*Würzburg sculptor,*
*Tombstone of Eberhard von Wolfskeel, about 1380*

ticed door at the exit is by the Würzburg craftsman Nikolaus Neeb, about 1712, and is in its original position.

## Bulwark (13)

The impressive, twin-naved bulwark with its massive vaults supported by solid columns has been transformed into a treasure trove of works of art and craftmanship.

*Near the entrance:* ● Late gothic table with richly carved oak legs from the town hall in Würzburg by Tilman Riemenschneider, 1506; top is of Solnhofen stone bearing the coats of arms of the Prince-Bishop, Lorenz von Bibra (1456–1519) of Würzburg, of the Bishop Gabriel von Eyb (1447–1535) of Eichstätt, who presented the stone to the town, and of the town of Würzburg.

*On the left:* Panel paiting "Virgin clothed in robes of grain", Swabian master, about 1450. Sacristy cupboard from Künzelsau, 2nd half 15th century. Limewood relief "Death of the Virgin", Franconian-Swabian master, about 1515. St. Valentine, Riemenschneider school, about 1505. Limewood relief "Adoration of the Magi", Franconian-Swabian master, beginning of 16th century.

*1st wall case on the left:* silver and gold-plated tankards and 17th and 18th century silverware. Including: Owl Cup, goblet in the form of an owl, unknown craftsman from Wertheim, about 1660. Two goblets with lids from the Würzburg millers' guild, by the Augsburg goldsmith, Philipp Stenglin (1667–1744), 1715 and an unknown Augsburg master, 1700. – ● Large tankard with lid, made for the barrel-makers' guild in Würzburg, by Gottfried Bischoff (1699–1737), Würzburg, 1735. Goblet of the Kitzingen barrelmakers' guild, 1639, added to in 1691, Kitzingen master craftsman. Chocolatière, gold-plated silver tray with Meißen china cup and engraved tumbler, by Johann Jacob Adam (about 1720–1791), Augsburg, 1757/58. Gold-plated silver beaker with snakeskin ornamention by various craftsmen.

**64**    *Tilman Riemenschneider, table from the town hall, 1506*

*Case in centre:* see page 76 ff.

Portrait of the Mayor of Würzburg, Caspar Eck, by an unknown Würzburg artist, 1577. Cabinet from Hopferstadt, last 3rd of 17th century. On the cabinet, a number of pewter screwcap bottles and storage jars, 17th–19th centuries. Portrait of Johann Eck, who emigrated from Würzburg to Kitzingen during the Counter-Reformation, by the Kitzingen painter Hans Heinisch, 1609. Small iron chest, 17th century. Alabaster relief "Throne of Grace", from the Round Church in the Marienberg Fortress, Würzburg, by Michael Kern (1580–1649), about 1605.

*2nd wall case of the left:* Silver and gold-plated goblets and 16th–18th century silverware. Includes, from ● silver treasure hidden in Würzburg during the Thirty Years' War, a silver, partly gold-plated woman's belt, by the Würzburg goldsmith, Ulrich Scherer, end of 16th century, also two goblets by Philipp Breuning (died after 1630), Würzburg, about 1620, and an aquilegia goblet by the Nuremberg master, Hans auf der Burg (died 1615), about 1600. ● Large, twin goblets, known as the "Doppelscheuer", by Thomas Stoer the Elder (died 1611), Nuremberg, about 1600. Bezoar stone from a horse belonging to Countess Sophia von Schönborn, who had the gold-plated silver foot with inscription and coat of arms made in 1725 by an unknown Augsburg goldsmith. ● Grape goblet, by Hans Petzold (born 1551), Nuremberg, beginning 17th century; two goblets with lids by the Nuremberg craftsmen Peter Wiber (died 1641) and Hans Berthold, (1st half 17th century); a hardwood goblet with silver decoration, south German, beginning 17th century (all lent by the Bayerische Hypotheken- und Wechselbank of Munich). On the back wall: crozier from the Cistercian Abbey in Ebrach for the office of Herlheim, decorated with monastery coat of arms, boar with abbot's crozier, 1683.

*Thomas Stoer the Elder: Twin gilded silver goblet,
known as "Doppelscheuer", about 1600*

Putto with coat of arms of the thanes of Steinruck, from the
epitaph of the Prince-Bishop of Bamberg and Dean of the
Cathedral of Würzburg, Neidhard von Thüngen (1545–1598)
in the Cathedral of Würzburg, by Hans Juncker (1582–about
1623), about 1600. Small iron chest, 17th century. Portrait
of the Prince-Bishop of Würzburg and Bamberg, Johann Gottfried von Aschhausen (1575–1621) by an unknown artist,
about 1620. Cabinet from Hueberspflege in Würzburg, last

third 17th century. On top of the cabinet a number of bronze mortars, 16th–17th centuries. Portrait of the Prince-Bishop of Würzburg and Bamberg, Franz von Hatzfeld (1596–1642), by an unknown artist, about 1640. Large oil painting "The market place in Würzburg with the Marienkapelle", by Oswald Onghers (1628–1706), last third 17th century. Figure of an angel with incense holder, Franconian, about 1600.

*3rd wall case on the left:* Ecclesiastical gold and silver objects from the baroque era. Includes a chalice from the Bürgerspital in Würzburg, by Johann Christian Pfister (1703–1768), Würzburg, about 1750. ● Chalice from the former Benedictine Abbey of St. Stephan's, Würzburg, by the Augsburg goldsmith, Georg Ignaz Bauer (died 1790), 1775/77. Chalice from the former Cistercian Monastery Maria Bildhausen by a goldsmith, N.B. from Neustadt/Saale, 1749. Lavabo with water and wine holders from St. Stephan's in Würzburg by Caspar Xaver Stippeldey (1735–1808), Augsburg, 1775/77. Lavabo with water and wine holder from Stift Haug, Würzburg, by Franz Christoph Mederle (died 1765), Augsburg, 1755/57. By the same artist a ● silver relief "Christ Falls beneath the Cross", Augsburg, 1749/51. On the back wall, wall console carved in wood for a (lost) figure of St. John Nepomuk with original mounting, about 1750.

At the end of the room, entrance to Kilian's Hall (14). A continuation of the tour of bulwark (13) after room 14 (see p. 75).

## St. Kilian's Room (14)

This room corresponds to the Knights' Hall at the southern end of the bulwarks and is situated in the north corner bastion of the Echter defences. In the showcases, ecclesiastical artefacts from the earliest days of the bishopric to baroque times are on display. The late gothic panel-paintings depict the life, work and martyr's deaths of the Franconian Apostles, St. Kilian and his companions, Kolonat and Totnan.

*Right:* The large showcase contains paraments and ecclesiastical items dating from the 15th to the 18th centuries. These include: two wooden ciboria from the Church of St. Kunigund in Burgerroth (15th century); a chasuble embroidered with gold and silver threads and showing scenes of the sufferings and death of Christ, from the parish church of Unterschei-

*"Eagle Flight of Alexander the Great", South German, silk embroidery, late 10th century*

chach (16th century); the wooden crook of an abbot's crosier found in a grave in the former Benedictine abbey of St. Stephan in Würzburg (17th century); a wooden, originally gilded monstrance with crystallised quartz (15th century). Furthermore, you can also see the following items; • two chasubles made from pressed, embossed and decorated leather with matching stoles and maniples from the parish church of Gänheim and from the chapel of the former "Hospital for Incurables" in Würzburg (2nd half of 18th century); a model of Christ as a child, made of coloured wax and with glass eyes, the model was made in a Franconian monastery ca. 1750/60 and comes from the pilgrimage church at Fährbrück; and finally a chasuble with stole maniple and bursa, "Gros de Tours" stitched with silver thread and coloured silk (2nd half of 18th century). Copperplate engraving "The Glory of St. Kilian and his Companions" by Johann Adam Delsenbach (1687–1765) based on a painting which later disappeared, by Johann Michael Rottmayr (1664–1730) in the Dorothee Church in Vienna, 1712. • Silk embroidery on linen depicting "The Eagle Flight of Alexander the Great", the work was carried out in south Germany and based on Byzantine models, late 10th century; the embroidery was originally sewn on the back of the Kilian flag which can still be seen in the entrance hall (21 b) of the museum. A page out of the "Prosapassional" which was manufactured in Nuremberg at the end of the 14th century with a coloured wood-engraving of the death of St. Kilian, printed by Günther Zainer in Augsburg, 1471/72. An incunabulum print of "Antiphonarium Herbipolense" with the hymn to St. Kilian, Würzburg 1499.

*In a showcase in the window-recess on the right:* • Bronze candlestick inlaid with silver, from the parish church in Stetten, it is the work of a Lotharingian silversmith in the second half of the 11th century. Bronze cross – an archaeological find from Lauda, 12th century. • Bronze door-handle shaped like a lion's head, from a portal of Würzburg Cathedral and made

*"The Martyrdom of St. Kilian and his two Companions"
painted by a Nuremberg master about 1475*

in a workshop in Mainz around 1050 (on loan from the Cathedral authorities). Three lions' heads made of gilded copper, 11/12th century. Gilded copper pyxes decorated with sunk enamel from a church in Krausenbach/Spessart; the work was done in Limoges in the 13th century.

*On the end wall:* ● The panel-painting "The Life of St. Kilian and his Companions" which was painted by a Nuremberg Master circa 1475, from the Church of St. Lorenz in Nuremberg and which shows, in the background, the oldest view of the Marienberg in Würzburg.

*In the wall-showcase:* Ecclesiastical gold and silver objects dating from the Gothic period and including the following items: a chalice made by Bartholomäus Ways from Regensburg in 1492 and donated to the parish church in Unteraltertheim in 1654; ● crystallised quartz reliquary for a thorn from Christ's crown of thorns, made in Venice ca. 1330, the silver-plated setting was probably made by the Nuremberg goldsmith, Albrecht Glim ca. 1500; this precious reliquary comes from the old church in the Marienberg Fortress in Würzburg and was later to be found in the Court Chapel of the Residenz (on loan from the Bayerische Verwaltung der Staatlichen Schlösser, Gärten und Seen); ● a reliquary for a splinter from the Cross made by an unknown craftsman in Nuremberg ca. 1510; this reliquary was donated by the Prince Bishop, Lorenz von Bibra (1456–1519) and comes from the circular church in the fortress of Marienberg or the Cathedral and was later to be found in the Court Chapel of the Residenz in Würzburg (on loan from the Bayerische Verwaltung der Staatlichen Schlösser, Gärten und Seen); five chalices dating from the 14th to 15th centuries; ● ornate silver censer made in 1420 by either a Würzburg or a Nuremberg master craftsman, from the former Augustinian monastery in Würzburg; four small silver-plated figures representing the prophets, made by an unknown craftsman in the 15th-century; a ciborium, made of gilded copper, part of the original decoration of the "Marienkapelle" in Würzburg, ca. 1470. At the back of the case there are three processional crosses dating from the 14th to the 16th centuries. On the wall above the showcase there are three keystones which depict St. Kilian, Kolonat and Totnan. These were the work of an unknown sculptor in Würzburg (ca. 1485) and came originally from the chapel of the former canon's resi-

*Silver censer made by a Franconian craftsman, ca. 1420*

dence – Rödelsee – in Würzburg. This chapel was desecrated in 1865. You can also see the altarpiece "The Life of St. Jacob" painted by an artist from the central Rhineland in the first third of the 16th century (on loan from the Bayerische Nationalmuseum in Munich) and a limewood figure of St. Stephen, Franconian, ca. 1525.

*Left:* Limewood figure of St. Urban, Franconian ca. 1525. South German panel-painting showing "Pontius Pilate presenting Christ" and dating from the 2nd half of the 15th century. Sandstone relief pietà bearing the coat of arms of the Würzburg mayor, Georg Ganzhorn; the relief was produced in the

Riemenschneider workshop ca. 1510. Three bells dated 1442, 1665 and 1714. Panel-painting of St. Kilian, the work of an artist from Main Franconia, ca. 1520 (on loan from the Bayerische Nationalmuseum in Munich). Carved figure of Christ riding on a donkey, from South Germany, early 16th century. On the wall above it, Gothic tracery dating from the 14th century. Furthermore, a panel-painting "The Life of St. Kilian and his Companions" painted by an unknown Würzburg artist in 1626; it first hung in the Cathedral and after 1659 it was in the "Hospital for Incurables" on the Steinberg.

*In the showcase on the left:* Ecclesiastical gold and silver objects dating from the Renaissance and baroque periods including the following: a ciborium from the Käppele in Würzburg, made around 1720 by the Würzburg goldsmith, Johann Kiehl who died in 1742; a chalice from the former "Hofspital" church in Würzburg, made by Caspar Riß von Rissenfeld, a craftsman from Augsburg who died in 1712; ● a ciborium made by Georg Müller (died in 1632) ca. 1625 in Würzburg, a donation from the Würzburg Prince-Bishop, Philipp Adolf von Ehrenberg (1583–1631), to the Reuerer monastery; a ciborium from the Käppele in Würzburg, made by the local goldsmith, Georg Anton Lanius the Younger (1682–1725), at the beginning of the 18th century; ● two large altar candelabra depicting, St. Kilian and the Marienberg Fortress, made by Johann Kaiser in Würzburg in 1663 and donated by Johann Philipp von Schönborn (1605–1673), Archbishop of Mainz and Prince-Bishop of Würzburg, to the chapel of the Marienberg Fortress (on loan from the Bayerische Verwaltung der Staatlichen Schlösser, Gärten und Seen). Two silver and gold-plated embossed copper figures of St. Ignatius and St. Aloysius, early 18th century.

*On the wall above the showcase:* The coat of arms of the dean of Würzburg's cathedral, Kilian von Bibra. This coat of arms was made by an unknown craftsman in Würzburg ca. 1485 and comes from the former canon's residence – Rödelsee –

in Würzburg. There is also an altarpiece "St. Kilian and St. Nicholas" painted by a Franconian artist ca. 1465 (on loan from the Bayerische Nationalmuseum in Munich). Limewood figure of St. Thomas carved by a sculptor in Nuremberg who worked with Veit Stoß (before 1450–1533), dated ca. 1520.

*On the pillar in the middle of the room:* A statue from Höchberg showing the Virgin Mary with Child made by a Würzburg craftsman, ca. 1480.

From here the tour continues through the Bulwark (13) along the east (window) side.

## Bulwark (13) continued

*Left:* ● Silver-plated crown of a processional flag, the so-called "Viermännerfahne" (Four Men's Flag) which belonged to the Citizens' Sodality (religious group of laymen and clergy) and was made in 1743–45 by the Augsburg goldsmiths, Franz Thaddäus Lang (ca. 1693–1773) and David Theodor Saler (1706–1763). In a niche in the wall a statue of the Virgin Mary from the central Rhineland ca. 1750. Silver-plated crown of a processional flag made by an unknown craftsman ca. 1750. Sandstone pulpit from the church at Oberwerrn with reliefs of St. Kilian and St. Valentine, as well as the coat of arms of Prince-Bishop Julius Echter von Mespelbrunn (1545–1617), dated 1601. Figure of St. Nicholas with an offertory box, made by an unknown sculptor in Würzburg and donated to the "Ehehaltenhaus" in Würzburg in 1659. Large oil painting of "The Birth of Christ", Franconian ca. 1590, donated by Johann Wilhelm and Maria Katharina Schein to the pilgrimage church "Maria im Sande" near Dettelbach.

*First window-recess:* Pewter engraving of the Virgin Mary by an unknown craftsman, F.A.H. in 1694. Copperplate engraving "Würzburg encircled by its baroque bastions" by Johann Ulrich Kraus (1655–1719) based on a drawing by Johann Michael Maucher (1645–1701); the engraving was used as the lower part of the Würzburg calendar issued between 1696 and

1729. In the *showcase* you can see various keys dating from the 8th to the 17th centuries.

Foundation-stone slab from the bastions of St. Burkard, part of Würzburg's town wall fortifications, 1675. Portrait of Johann Philipp von Schönborn (1605–1673), Archbishop of Mainz and Prince Bishop of Würzburg, who had the town's baroque fortifications built.

*Second window-recess:* The showcase contains a choice selection of Franconian medals and decorations. The most interesting are: ● the Order of St. Joseph from the grand duchy of Würzburg, donated in 1807 by the Grand Duke Ferdinand (1769–1824); the Phoenix Order, the Hohenlohe family order, donated in 1758 by Prince Philipp Ernst of Hohenlohe-Schillingsfürst (1663–1759); the Foundation Cross of "St. Anna's Grand-Ducal Foundation for Unmarried Ladies" in Würzburg, founded in 1811 and dissolved in 1814; ● a medal of the Würzburg Prince-Bishop, Lorenz von Bibra (1456–1519), this was the first German cast medal and the casting mould was possibly made by Tilman Riemenschneider (ca. 1460–1531), dated 1511 and 1515 respectively; ● a magnificent series of medals of Prince-Bishop Johann Philipp von Greiffenclau (1652–1719), commemorating the good harvest of 1706 and made by Georg Hautsch (1664–1736) from Nuremberg; ● a large lead medal of the Canon of Bamberg, Willibald von Redwitz, made in Würzburg in 1536 by Peter Dell the Elder (ca. 1490–1552); a medal commemorating the marriage of Wilhelm Ganzhorn to his wife, Sabine, née Maier, made by an unknown medal-engraver in Würzburg in 1539; a medal made in Augsburg in 1712 to mark the jubilee of the Elector of Mainz, Lothar Franz von Schönborn (1655–1729) as the Canon of Würzburg – this medal was made by Philipp Heinrich Müller (1654–1719).

*Central showcase opposite:* Jewish ritual objects from Franconia including the following: 7 Torah scrolls showing the symbols for the religious holidays; several besomin containers, among them one which was probably made in Vienna ca. 1740 and which unfortunately was damaged in the fire on 16th March, 1945; numerous Chanukkah candlesticks and ceremonial plates.

Portrait of Duke Bernhard von Sachsen-Weimar (1604–1639), who, after the death of the Swedish king, Gustav Adolf (1594–1632), held the duchy of Franconia as a Swedish fief from 1633 to 1634. Feudal lord's chair from Schernau Castle, early 17th century. Portrait of Eberhard von Lichtenstein painted by an unknown Würzburg artist in 1626; Lichtenstein was the only canon to remain in Würzburg and in 1631 he saved the town from being looted by the Swedes and also refunded a large part of the forced contributions from his own fortune.

*Third window-recess:* A leaflet showing how the Swedes took the town of Würzburg and the Marienberg Fortress, 1631. Copperplate engraving depicting a view of the Marienberg Fortress by Johann Leypolt in 1604. In the *showcase* you can see a collection of various official and decorative keys dating from the 17th and 18th centuries.

*Centre case opposite:* standard measures and measuring rods from Würzburg, dating from the 15th to the 19th centuries, including two standard measures for grain, 1475, three standard measures for salt, 1511, and one measure dated 1530 – the so-called "quarter-head".

● Portrait of King Gustav Adolf of Sweden (1594–1632), a drawing in red chalk done in 1632 by Lorenz Strauch (born 1554); the troops commanded by Gustav Adolf succeeded in capturing the Marienberg Fortress by storming the Echter bulwarks on 18th October, 1631. Small iron chest dating from the 17th century. ● Five sandstone Caesar reliefs which were made in 1604 by the Swiss sculptor, Sebastian Götz, and taken from the bartizan of the circular church in the Marienberg Fortress – this turret was pulled down in 1814.

*Centre showcase opposite:* Pottery and earthenware from the 16th and 17th centuries including: ● a large colourfully glazed tankard with a raised Crucifixion group, with Adam and Eve on the sides and underneath, Christ entering Jerusalem and the Adoration of the Magi – this tankard was made in Nuremberg ca. 1548 in the workshop of Paulus Preuning (ca. 1526–after 1593); also Creußen stoneware from the 17th century; one particularly interesting item is the large tankard, adorned with the Apostles, which was made for Hanns Hartmann von und zu Erffa, a captain at the Veste (castle) in Coburg, in 1638. Furthermore, you can see two tall Siegburg drinking mugs made by Hans Hilgers in 1577 and 1578. Bottom row: 17th-century stoneware from Creußen and Saxony and a small earthen jug decorated with Veronica's sudarium, Franconian ca. 1550.

Portrait of Prince Bishop Philipp Adolf von Ehrenberg (1583–1631) by an unknown Würzburg artist, ca. 1625. Small iron chest, 17th century.

*Fourth window-recess:* Wall tile bearing the coat of arms of Prince-Bishop Julius Echter von Mespelbrunn (1545–1617), made in 1574. Earthenware relief also showing Echter's coat of arms. In the *showcase* there are astronomic calendars and sun-clocks of the Renaissance and baroque periods.

*Centre showcase opposite:* pewterware dating from the 15th to the 18th centuries, ● including a magnificent bowl, called the "Temperantia Bowl", modelled on the work of François Briot (ca. 1560–ca. 1616) – the cast was moulded in 1611 by Caspar Enderlein (1566–1633) and the bowl was cast by Michael Hermersam (ca. 1596–1658) ca. 1630; a jug made by an unknown craftsman in the 15th or 16th century and found in the River Main near Haßfurt. One exhibit is the pouring jug probably used during meetings of the town council in Gerolzhofen; this was one of a series of twelve jugs originally

*Stoneware tankard showing the Apostles, Creußen, 1638*

(another of this series is on display in Room 11), which were made by an unknown tinsmith in Nuremberg at the beginning of the 16th century. Finally, there are also various serpentine-vessels with pewter mountings, 16th/17th century.

Portrait of Mathias Held, privy councillor to the Kaiser and vice-chancellor, painted by an unknown artist ca. 1550. Portrait of the mayor of Würzburg, Georg Ganzhorn, also painted by an unknown artist in Würzburg in 1538. Folding stool, first half of the 16th century. Embroidery "St. Jacob", antependium from (Spitalkirche) in Karlstadt, 1519.

*Fifth window-recess:* Limewood relief of St. Katharina, made in South Germany ca. 1540. In the two *showcases* you can see pocket watches from the 16th to the 19th centuries and Franconian pocket watches dating back to the 18th and 19th centuries, among these are some made by the most important watch-maker in Würzburg, Johann Henner (1676–1756).

*Centre showcase opposite:* Table-clocks, sun-clocks and astronomical instruments etc. from the 16th to the 18th centuries including: ● a "clock on an inclined plane" made in Strasbourg, ca. 1680, by Isaak Habrecht (1611–1686); a towershaped table clock made by Johann Michael Brügel in Würzburg ca. 1680; ● astronomical instruments such as a compass rose, a lunar clock, a compass, a sun-clock and a calendar made by Christoph Schißler the Elder (ca. 1531–1608) in Augsburg in 1557; a declinatorium for measuring the magnetic variation of the compass, made by Georg Friedrich Brander (1713–1784) in Augsburg in 1770.

Limewood group – "The Adoration of the Magi" carved by a craftsman from Nuremberg, ca. 1510. St. Sebastian figure made by a craftsman who worked with Riemenschneider and dated ca. 1510. Panel-painting of "Christ and the Samaritan woman at the well" by Lucas Cranach the Elder (1472–1553) in 1532 (on loan from the Federal Republic of Germany and formerly belonging to the German Reich). Panel-painting of "Adam and Eve" by Lucas Cranach the Elder, ca. 1515 (on loan from the Fed. Republic of Germany and formerly the property of the German Reich). Commode from South Germany, 1513. Figure of Mary, (figure of the Christ Child is missing) from the Odenwald, 1454.

*Our tour continues up the winding staircase to the*

# Department of Folk Art (16 & 17)

Apart from the variety of everyday implements on display here, old Franconian regional costumes, in particular those from the Ochsenfurt Gau (area), with the elaborate matching folk jewellery are especially interesting. You can also see rustic furniture mainly from Hohenlohe-Franconia with its attractive hand-painted decoration.

*In the staircase:* Two 16th century brass bowls. The sandstone coat of arms of Prince Bishop Julius Echter von Mespelbrunn (1545–1617), 1575. Franconian votive picture, 1807. The dungeon door from a prince-bishop's palace in the Rhön, 16th century. The child-portraits of Christian Wilhelm von Gleichen and Wilhelm Ernst von Gleichen painted by an unknown artist ca. 1675.

*In the Folk Art Department,* the first room you reach from the winding staircase on the left is the *"Obere Diele"* (*upper hall*) above the southern bulwark (16).

*By the stairs:* The richly ornate rococo shaft of a wayside shrine from Gabolshausen in Grabfeld, Franconian, ca. 1760. Processional signs depicting the Mysteries of the Rosary, Franconian ca. 1800.

*Upstairs, in the hall to the right of the entrance:* Franconian loom, 1839, the loom is threaded and a piece of weaving has been started to show how the loom functions. Next to it, there is a small cloth-press, ca. 1800. On the wall there are blocks for printing cloth, 18th/19th centuries. A tailor's stove and the iron which went with it, 2nd third of the 19th century.

*In the corner:* two early types of bicycles: a walking machine and a high bike, both made of wood and dating from the 19th century; a child's tricycle, 2nd half of the 19th century.

*Open fireplace:* Kitchen oven with kitchen implements of the 17th to 19th centuries including: a copper water-boiler and tub, as well as a barrel for "Sauerkraut", 19th century, (on the right of the oven). On top of the oven there is a bronze three-legged kettle, 16th century, a roasting jack and a stand for pots etc. On the mantle you can see a coffee-grinder, a mortar, a candlestick, oil-lamps and pewter candlesticks etc. To the left of the fireplace you can see a chopping board (1706) and cast brass scales, the masterpiece of Bankel in Nuremberg in 1800. Large glazed pottery pastry bowl, early 19th century. On the wall there are copper baking tins – 18th to 19th centuries.

On the seat in front of the oven there is a coffee-roaster, a baking dish and a copper fish kettle, 19th century.

On the tables in front of the oven there are more kitchen implements including a fish kettle and a food carrier, pewter from Ansbach ca. 1780, as well as a wasp trap.

*In the corner* the massive baroque staircase from the house at Marktplatz 2, Karlstadt am Main, which was built in 1721.

*On the left of the stairs:* ● Hand-painted four-poster bed by Johann Michael Rössler (1791–1849) from Untermünkheim near Schwäbisch Hall, later in the Franconian Odenwald in 1844. In the bed you can see so-called bed "carriage" for straightening the bedcovers and for the bedpan, 19th century. To the left: a cupboard for Maria Katharina Klaus, from Untermünkheim, made by Johann Michael Rössler in 1829, as well as a Franconian hand-painted cradle, 1834.

*Next to the window:* a 19th century Good Friday rattle; these rattles are still used in Franconian villages nowadays instead of church bells to summon the villagers to church and to tell them the time of day in the Holy Week. In front of the window there is a beehive-shaped drying oven for juniper berries and herbs, from the Capuchin monastery of the Käppele in Würzburg, ca. 1800.

*On the trestle:* waffle irons and irons for making consecrated wafers/hosts from the 16th to the 18th centuries, including: (2nd waffle iron from the front) with a picture of the Virgin Mary and a coat of arms, 1549; a waffle iron with a picture

*Figurine wearing a traditional Ochsenfurt costume for special occasions*

of St. George (1717) – (4th from the front); a wafer iron for making large wafers (used in Mass) and small wafers (for Communion) – (3rd from the back) and finally a waffle iron with pictures of Adam and Eve, 18th century (1st from the back).

*Further left:* Flour chest from the Rhön, ca. 1800. Bread baskets and chopping board from 1816.

*In the corner opposite the entrance:* Table with pewter ware and kitchen cupboard, with a cook in a traditional costume from Hohenlohe Franconia ca. 1840.

*On the left side of the wall:* Large oven; iron chest showing scenes from the Bible; terracotta stand with imperial busts ca. 1700, from the former house of Bildhausen Monastery in Unsleben near Neustadt a.d. Saale.

*Next to the oven:* elaborately painted cradle, 2nd half of the 17th century. Rocking-horse from the castle at Ellrichshausen a.d. Jagst ca. 1700. Richly carved bedstead from Schwebenried near Schweinfurt as well as a night chair, early 19th century.

*On the wall:* Warming pan, 18th century and school blackboard ca. 1850. Two examples of "verre églomisé" – a technique of painting on the reverse side of glass panes. The pictures show "Mary, Help of Christians" and "St. Joseph" from Oberammergau, 19th century.

*Near the door:* Three ornate wrought-iron graveyard crosses from Franconia, late 18th and early 19th centuries.

In the *centre of the room:* The showcase displays ● festive regional costumes from the Ochsenfurt Gau (area), figurines by Heinz Schiestl (1867–1940) and traditional jewellery, as well as knitted and patterned stockings. On the central pillar: embroidered decorative towels including one with elaborate satin stitch embroidery, 1709, and painted woodenboxes, 18th century.

*On the ceiling:* Traditional guild signs and an iron inn-sign as well as the crest of a processional pole encircled by acanthus leaves, ca. 1700.

*Take the stairs back to the lower hall (17)*

*In the left part of the room behind the balustrade:* Large chest with the coats of arms of Franconian families, 16th century.

Above: gallery with scenes from a Franconian picture-bible, ca. 1600.

*1st and 2nd table showcases:* Jewellery, fans and games from a patrician house in Würzburg, 19th century.

*On the left along the wall:* ● Large hand-painted cupboard with rural scenes – allegories of the Four Elements, from Wunsiedel, 1755. Other painted cupboards from Hohenlohe-Franconia, 1836, and Swabia, 1793. In between them are chests from Hohenlohe Franconia and the Rhön. Carved clothespresses of the 17th to 19th centuries, yokes from the 18th to 19th centuries and marzipan moulds of the baroque and Biedermeier periods. Cast-iron stove from Ebelsbach am Main, probably made in Laufach in Spessart ca. 1770.

*3rd table showcase:* Moulds, craftsmen's implements and the signets of Franconian guilds from the 14th to 18th centuries.

*4th table showcase:* Cutlery and christening spoons from the 17th to 19th centuries.

*5th table showcase:* Prayer-leaders' staffs, burial and storm crucifixes, rosaries and pilgrimage pictures from Franconia, 18th to 19th centuries.

*6th table showcase:* Franconian costume jewellery, prayer-book clasps and elaborately decorated prayer-books, early 19th century.

*7th table showcase:* Rosaries and hand-painted religious pictures of the rococo period from Franconia.

At the end of the hall: ● a rococo apothecary's shop from Dettelbach am Main, with ornate carving and a hand-carved trellis over the counter probably made by the Dettelbach sculptor, Johann Michael Becker (1703–1777) ca. 1745/50. Scales, mortar and pestle and other shop equipment. On the left: two indentures for merchant's apprentices as well as Bad Kissingen's oldest list of spa visitors, dated 1788.

**85**

*To the right of the shop* is the entrance to the ● Vinegrower's Parlour (18) from Sulzfeld am Main. This room has hand-painted wooden panelling as well as a decorated ceiling from the time around 1590. Franconian terracotta stove with a cast iron fire-box from the "Post Inn" in Burgwindheim, 1776. On the tables there is Franconian pewterware etc. On the shelf to the right you can see mainly stoneware vessels from Saxony, Westerwald and Creußen in Upper Franconia in particular. On top of the large chest near the entrance there is a pewter jug dated 1740 which belonged to the Bakers' Guild and a candle-maker's pot for making dipped candles, 1662. On the same wall as the stove there is a wrought iron painted wall-clock, 1st half of the 17th century.

Next you come to the *inn parlour* from the "Adler Inn" in Junkersdorf in Haßberge (18a) ca. 1760, with its carved benches, serving hatch and wall cupboard. Table-top clock by Johann Joseph Langschwert (1712–1783), a clockmaker from Würzburg, dated ca. 1750/60. A green glazed rococo stove ca. 1750. On the left pillar: clay figure of "Virgin with Child" from Bad Mergentheim ca. 1770. Next to it: an oil painting "Quodlibet", a wall display of letters with five naturalistic, painted pieces of writing, including a promissory note concerning a vineyard in Würzburg, by Cornelius Biltius (born in 1653), 1682. Faïence crucifix, 19th century.

The next room is the *Biedermeier room* (18b) with wallpaper showing rural motifs, made by a Parisian manufacturer ca. 1790, from Randersacker. In the suspended cradle (ca. 1830) there is a set of christening clothes with fine lace, ca. 1800. Cast iron round stove with reliefs representing the saga of Hercules among other things, ca. 1800, from the Mainsondheim Castle near Dettelbach am Main. "Pyramid" piano by Johann Caspar Schlimbach (1777–1861) ca. 1830 (on loan from the Deutsche Museum in Munich).

Hall (18c). ● Here is a large showcase for costumes including extremely colourful costumes from the Ochsenfurt Gau (area);

*Vintner's Parlour from Sulzfeld, ca. 1590*

on the left, a lady's costume from the Rhön; on the right,
a lady's costume from Opferbaum; in the middle, a man's
costume from the Schweinfurt Gau (area) with its red
waistcoat, 1855, and a man's costume from the Spessart with
its long green jacket, ca. 1850. On the showcase there are three
carved stands for costume hats.

*In the showcase opposite:* an exquisite selection of earthenware
figures made by Aschaffenburg-Damm manufactory. To mention just a few: ● the large group of the Chinese Emperor
ca. 1850/60, shaped using the hollow mould of Johann Peter

Melchior (1742–1825) – this mould was previously used by Höchst, the porcelain manufacturers; the small sultan figure and the Turkish musicians. On the left: stoneware crockery and glasses of the Biedermeier period.

*At the end of the room:* hand-painted wardrobe for Johann Georg Heighold from the district of Untermünkheim/Hohenlohe, made by Johann Michael Rössler (1791–1849) in 1828. Pictorial clock with views of Würzburg from the north, ca. 1810. Chest for a young woman's trousseau, from Hohenlohe Franconia, 1811.

Take the stairs to the northern bulwark-tower: on the right, there are two collage pictures depicting "October" and "December" – both so-called "Mussiv" paintings by Johann Heinrich Zang (1733–1811), in 1795 and 1807. *Artisans' room* (18 d) ● with a cooper's workshop, in working order and fully equipped. On the right: a guild chest, 1706; signet dated 1640 and a book, which was started in 1706, tracing the history of master-coopers in Würzburg.

*In the corridor* outside the balustrade on the way *back to the winding staircase:* Large iron stove with the coat of arms of the Prince-Bishop of Fulda, Heinrich von Bibra (1759–1788) from Weißendorf Castle, near Neustadt an der Aisch. Large scales from Neustadt/Saale, 1701.

*On the outside wall (window-side):* ● Pictures of regional costumes from Lower Franconia; coloured lithographs by Peter Geist (1816–1867), 1852. Hand-painted cupboards from Hohelohe Franconia, mostly the work of Johann Michael Rössler, 1st half of the 19th century.

*In the middle of the corridor:* ● large collection of magnificently coloured examples of "verre églomisé" (a technique of painting on the reverse of glass-panes) from South Germany, Augsburg, Oberammergau, Staffelsee, Bayerische Wald, the Black Forest, the southwest part of Germany and Franconia, primarily 19th century.

Furthermore, two Franconian hand-painted cupboards, 1835

and 1807. Small Franconian chest dated 1779. A small house-altar with a "Prague figure of Jesus as a child", from Iphofen ca. 1760. Two portraits of the mother and wife of Andreas Müller, an engineer-captain and architect in Würzburg, one dated early 18th century and the other dated 1742.

*At the end of the corridor:* to the right of the door, a hand-painted wardrobe by Johann Michael Rössler in Untermünk-heim. Next to it, is a pilgrimage picture of the Miracle of Vierzehnheiligen, from the Capuchin monastery at Karlstadt, 2nd half of the 18th century. In the small corner-cupboard, figure of Christ as a child made out of wax, ca. 1760, next to it, Maria Immaculata in an ornate rococo shrine.

To continue the tour, take the winding stairs down (15) towards the exit (View of the second courtyard with its horse-pond and the Scherenberg Gateway). Limewood figure of "Christ's Scourging at the Pillar", Franconian ca. 1750. Sandstone coat of arms of Johann Ulrich Zollner, 1671.

## Lower Bulwarks (19)

The former stables of the Fortress now serve as a museum for objects dating from prehistoric times and from the early days of Lower Franconia. This exhibition of over 2000 objects spans the period from the Paleolithic Age to the late Middle Ages.

*Showcase 1:* Tools and objects dating from the Paleolithic and Mesolithic Age (100000–5000 B.C.). The oldest tool is a celt from the Paleolithic Age from Oberschwappach, underneath – a collection of treated and shaped microliths from the Mesolithic Age, found near Grosslangheim and on the top of the Schwanberg near Kitzingen: triangular and crosscut arrowheads, different scrapers and scratchers.

*Showcase 2:* Pottery from the Neolithic Age (5000–4000 B.C.). On the left – the oldest articles made from clay, linear pottery: bell-shaped vessels, a very large storage vessel and a number of hanging storage vessels. Next to that, richly decorated pottery of the "Oberlauterbacher Group" and the "Rössener Culture", the latter was found mainly in a large village-settlement near Euerfeld.

*Showcase 3:* Pertains to rituals and cults of the dead in the Neolithic Age (5000–3000 B.C.). Below ● a unique find from Zeuzleben, 29 human teeth through which holes have been drilled, originally painted red, for use as a charm or amulet. Next to that – some completely new and unused tools to serve as offerings. At the top: richly decorated clay drum from a collective burial site near Grosseibstadt.

*Showcase 4:* Pottery from the late Neolithic Age (about 3000 B.C.). Finds from settlements of the "Michelsberg Culture": A very large storage vessel from Repperndorf, a baking dish, ladles, spoons, goblets and cups, primarily from Hopferstadt.

*Showcase 5:* Pottery from the Bell-Beaker culture (2500–1800 B.C.). Below: Corded pottery: an amphora from Grossostheim and numerous cups, mainly from the burial site near Bergrheinfeld. At the top: vessels from the "Glockenbecherkultur" – (Bell-Beaker culture), below that ● two especially beautifully shaped and completely decorated bell-beakers from Würzburg-Heidingsfeld.

*Showcase 6:* Technical innovations of the Neolithic Age. For each exemplary find there is an accompanying explanatory drawing to illustrate such inventions as spinning, weaving, pottery-making and the making·of stone tools or the building of houses.

*Showcase 7:* Tools of the late Neolithic period (3000–2000 B.C.). On the right-hand wall – stone and bone tools of the "Altheim culture" from the Altenberg near Burgerroth. On the left-hand wall: late Neolithic period tools out of amphibolite and silex, underneath, a semi-finished dagger from Gochsheim. At the bottom: late Neolithic period battle-axes of the "Michelsberg culture" and of the "Corded Ware culture".

*Showcase 8:* Finds from the Bronze Age (1800–1200 B.C.). At the bottom: weapons, tools and ornaments from the Bronze Age (tumulus period); at the top: vessels and pius from the middle and late Bronze Age. At the front – fragment of the bone of an upper-arm pierced by an arrowhead, out of a grave near Stetten.

*Showcase 9:* Ornaments from the late Bronze Age (1300–1200 B.C.). From a tumulus in Pflaumheim, all the ornaments of a very rich woman. ● Different kinds of ornaments such as spirals, rings, decorative pins, bronze and amber necklaces and numerous small caps which, going on the location of the find, were sewn onto a bonnet for decorative purposes. Various kinds of ornaments from a tumulus near Stettfeld.

*Showcase 10:* Hoards of the late Bronze Age (1300–1200 B.C.). Two hoards from Schweinfurt and Schwanberg consisting of three axes each, and a find from Niedernberg consisting of different tools such as axes, sickles or snaffles and various ornaments.

*Bell-shaped beakers, found in Würzburg-Heidingsfeld and Unterspiesheim (on the right), about 2000 B.C.*

*Showcase 11:* Hoards from the urnfield times (1200–750 B.C.). Sizable hoard-find from Reupelsdorf – bottom right. Next to this collection, the only recently discovered treasures from the elevated plain of the Bullenheim Hill take up a major portion of the display in this showcase. Display No. 3 is probably the most interesting and important. ● It consists of four axle-caps with axle-pins which are on the top adorned by a water-bird. They once belonged to a four-wheel cart or waggon. The only clue to the actual size of the waggon can be gotten from the reconstructed wooden wheel. It probably served as a ceremonial vehicle similar to the one for which a model was found at the burial grounds in Acholshausen in the "Kes-selwagengrab" (cauldron waggon grave) and which is on display in showcase 15. In front of the axle caps a flank-hilted sword (Hemigkofen type) a unique find which is nevertheless to be considered a treasure. Next to the hoards consisting exclusively of axes, the hoard-finds such as various pieces of equipment, tools, horse-gear, weapons and ornaments are also to be considered important. Top right: A pair of hanging ring ornaments, belonging to display No. 6, used as a chiming adornment for a wagon or a harness. Special mention should also be made of ● two embossed gold-foil fragments, belonging to hoard No. 5 (top left), part of a dish or cult cone, and bearing witness to the material wealth of their owners.

Also part of this ensemble – numerous tools among which an iron awl with a bone handle can be found and which is proof of the very early use of iron in this area.

*Showcase 12:* Ornaments and tools of the urnfield times (1200–750 B.C.). In the centre of the showcase wall – bronze burial offerings from a burial ground in Herlheim, dating from the very early urnfield era: neck-ornament, needles and differ-ent kinds of knives. To the left of that – special knife and a needle with a spherical head, from Niedernberg. To the right of that – a richly decorated neck ornament and a special knife, from Aub. Bottom – knives from urnfield times as well as a sandstone mould for a needle with a spherical head.

*Showcase 13:* Weapons of the urnfield times (1200–750 B.C.). Swords of different shapes: from the older urnfield times – a bronze-hilted sword from Herlheim and a flank-hilted sword (Hemigkofen type – Elsenfeld version) from Elsenfeld; from the younger urnfield times – different kinds of swords from Langenprozelten and Obertheres. Various bronze arrowheads and spearheads, some of which are decorated.

*Showcase 14:* The "cauldron waggon grave" from Acholshausen (about 1000 B.C.). This find, stemming from a cremational burial site represents a self-contained unit which is the grave of a male person, evidenced by the fact that spearheads were included as burial offerings. Additional bronze objects which are especially noteworthy: ● a bowl with handles, ● a cup and ● two ornately embossed discs, whose actual function is unclear. Next to that, numerous clay vessels of the Lower-Main-Swabian Group including bowls, dishes, cups, and pots with conical necks, as well as some rather squat-looking pottery from the Eastern Middle European region; one example of which is the very rare two-levelled vessel.

*Showcase 15a:* The "cauldron waggon" from Acholshausen (about 1000 B.C.). ● The miniature of a large waggon is the most important find from the burial place at Acholshausen. Following a tradition of the ancient Greeks, in times of drought the cauldron of a cult waggon or worship cart was probably struck so as to make it resound and thereby conjure up rain.

*Showcase 15b:* The sun cult in the urnfield times (1200–750 B.C.). The so-called sun-discs are interpreted as symbols of the sun. On display here – an especially magnificent one made of embossed gold-foil, from Goldbach, and two clay discs decorated with stamped imprints from Würzburg-Heidingsfeld and Fuchsstadt.

*Showcase 16:* Pottery from the urnfield times (1200–750 B.C.). Vessels of different shapes and sizes, among them, a large pot with a cylindrical neck from Essfeld (bottom right) and a rare two-levelled vessel from Grosslangheim (bottom left). Both date from the early urnfield times. Two vessels shaped like amphorae from Würzburg and a bulbous, red vessel with black painting from Pflaumheim (top right) stem from the later urnfield era.

*Showcase 17:* Ornaments of the Hallstatt period (750–450 B.C.). On the showcase-wall, right: ● the complete find from a woman's grave near Birkenfeld, consisting of neck-laces, toiletries (tweezers, nail cleaners and ear-curettes), fibulas, hanging ornament with rattling stones, bracelets, anklets. To the left of that: toiletries from Oberwaldbehrungen. From the same period, (on the showcase-wall, left) ornaments from a woman's grave near Birkenfeld. Above that, neck ornament and glassbead necklace from a woman's grave near Seifrieds-burg. Bottom left: some splendid specimens of hollow rings which were worn by women on their belts; in the centre – different types of fibulas, (on the right) neck ornaments, brace-lets, anklets and decorative buttons, all from a woman's grave near Merkershausen.

*Showcase 18:* Household equipment from the Hallstatt period (750–450 B.C.). Next to a large storage vessel for grain from Zellingen, two grindstones, the one in the back from Röttingen of the type "Napoleonshut" – (Napoleon's hat). In front – a funnel and a scoop, on the right – more cups and pots. Top right – some smaller vessels, among them a dish, richly

*Bronze cult waggon, found near Acholshausen,*
*about 1000 B.C.*

decorated with graphitic clay, from Örlenbach. Behind that – four clay weaving weights from a simple weaving loom.

*Showcase 19:* Trading articles of the Hallstatt period (750–450 B.C.). Top – ● an intricately decorated, thin-walled vessel with a conical neck from the large burial mound near Riedenheim. This precious object imported from a workshop located on the Upper-Danube River served the sovereign who was buried here as part of a valuable set of drinking vessels during his lifetime. ● 9 of the original 23 pointed iron bars weighing 4–5 kilogrammes, from a hoard near Aubstadt, which a wealthy dealer or craftsman buried there and later did not dig up again.

*Showcase 20:* Greek pottery from the Marienberg in Würzburg (530–470 B.C.). ● Some Greek pottery fragments, unearthed in the Fortress up on the Marienberg, are the only evidence left of some magnificent drinking vessels once owned by a local ruler. The fragments are from two craters (receptacles used for mixing water and wine) and three different drinking cups of the kind widely used at banquets in the days of ancient Greece. Such vessels with their typical black clay paint were produced in great numbers by the craftsmen in Athens.

*Showcase 21:* Pottery from the Hallstatt period (750–450 B.C.). Top – three ornate lids and various vessels. Bottom – doll's dishes from a burial mound near Schraudenbach; small toy figurines, probably used for board games; clay birds from Örlenbach and finally, three plates with sectioned-off areas, from Schwarzenau, Zeuzleben and Estenfeld.

*Showcase 22:* Weapons and ornaments from the Hallstatt period (750–450 B.C.). Flank-hilted swords from Westheim and Trimberg, the latter with a special tip-covering for the protection of the sword-tip, and two more such coverings (type – Oberwaldbehrungen). Bottom – two bronze sheets, originally fixed on belts, one of which is richly embossed and comes from Lindelbach.

*Showcase 23:* Celtic objects of the Latène period (450–100 B.C.). On the wall on the right – an iron knife from Kleinlangheim and a bone handle for the same kind of knife, from Lindelbach. Underneath – two vessels made on a potter's wheel with typical stamped decoration, from Schwebheim. On the centre of the showcase-wall – an iron sword with sheath, two rings and a spearhead from a grave near Rossbrunn and

*Doll's dishes, found in a child's grave near Schraudenbach, 6th century B.C.*

a sword with a handle in the shape of a person, from Margetshöchheim. On the showcase-wall on the left – various ornaments, among them, a neck ornament (finding-place unknown), a glass-bead necklace from Burggrumbach, bracelets and various fibulas. ● Bottom – ornaments from the early Latène period which were found in a woman's grave near Zeuzleben: a bronze, rolled, hollow ring neck ornamentation with clasp and a twisted neck ornamentation with clasp, two bracelets and a magnificent pin with a large coral head.

*Showcase 24:* Celtic objects from the Latène period (380–50 B.C.). On the showcase-wall, right – parts of a drinking horn; underneath, vessels made on a potter's wheel. An especially beautiful specimen is ● the bottle from Wenigumstadt. On the showcase-wall, left – the omega-shaped side of a horse-bit with bent-down bird-head tips, from Grosslangheim, and from the same location, a rein-holding ring, which was placed on a waggon as a guide for the straps. Underneath – fragments of Celtic bracelets made of glass and ● Celtic coins, popularly called "Regenbogenschüsselchen" (small rainbow bowls).

*Showcase 25:* Early Germanic objects (1st century B.C. – 1st century A.D.). Two clay situlae from Acholshausen and Baldersheim, underneath – a vessel, and weapons which have been bent out of shape in order to make them useless, found in Würzburg at a cremational burial site dating from the early 1st century, next to that, a vessel decorated with lines made by the teeth of a comb, from Baldersheim.

*Showcase 26:* Roman and Germanic metal objects (1st–4th century A.D.). On the showcase wall – numerous fibulas and other ornaments from every-day life. Top left – a bronze attachment in the shape of a young man with Dionysian attributes from Baldersheim, top right – from Hopferstadt, a vessel attachment in the shape of the head of Silenus, and between them, a very large enameled disc-shaped brooch which is still in excellent condition, from Frankenwinheim. Bottom of the showcase, left – three rein-holding rings from Roman waggons, an open-worked strap buckle from Geldersheim, depicting a dog chasing a hare, the back-end of a key, from Frankenwinheim and a skillet handle with a ram's head at the end, from Würzburg. In front – a miniature bronze statue of a dog, from Bimbach and of a ● billy-goat with two saddle-bags, from Frankenwinheim. To the right – a silver castings cake from Kreuzwertheim and a bronze mould for a fibula, from Geldersheim. In front – four Roman rings, including a silver ring with turquois coloured intaglio (engraved gem), depicting a Roman standard.

*Showcase 27:* Germanic pottery from the time of the Roman Empire (1st–4th century A.D.). From the cellar-like storage room of a merchant dealing in crockery during the 4th century in Essleben, numerous bottles and bowls made on a potter's

*Bronze dog and goat, found near Bimbach and Frankenwinheim, 1st/2nd century A.D.*

wheel (top left and centre of showcase). This kind of pottery is called "terra nigra" because of its very black glossy surface. Top right – a vessel with handles and a sieve (1st century) from Baldersheim.

*Showcase 28:* The Roman grave from Obernburg (about 200 A.D.). Left – ● gravestone, the urn with ashes, numerous jugs and vessels with handles, so-called "honey-pots", terra-sigillata vessels, a beaker, and fragments of large amphorae. In front – two iron objects used by sportsmen after working out to scrape the sweat, oil and dust from their bodies.

*Showcase 29:* Roman and Germanic finds from the time of the migration of peoples (4th–5th centuries A.D.). On the showcase-wall, right – numerous bronze objects from the Wettenburg. These were parts of Roman and Germanic garb, for example: belt-buckles, decorative trimmings, and fibulas. Further, a pendant in the shape of a small human-like head, perhaps with magic powers, a spoon and the bronze leg of a pail with an attachment in the shape of a human head. Underneath – a collection of coins, consisting of 135 Roman coins from late antiquity. Top left, on the showcase-wall: ● a silver

**99**

fibula and a silver bracelet from a woman's grave near Hammelburg. Next to that – a late-Roman terra-sigillata bowl, a decorated three-layer comb and ● two Gallo-Roman glass beakers, from a Germanic grave near Thüngersheim. Bottom left in the showcase: the complete find from a grave dating from the 5th century located in Kleinwallstadt. Underneath – a gold-plated silver fibula with delicate palmette decoration. To the right – a beaker from Baldersheim and a jug from Wenigumstadt.

*Showcase 30:* Ornaments and tools from the Merovingian period (450–700 A.D.). Numerous finds from the graveyards from the early Middle Ages in Kleinlangheim, Hellmitzheim and above all, Zeuzleben. Among the objects found are – a number of colourful clay and glassbead necklaces, almandine brooches, bird and snake brooches. An especially magnificent specimen ● – two gold-plated silver fibulas, worn as a pair, with Germanic animal ornamentation, from a woman's grave in Würzburg-Heidingsfeld and ● a silver brooch, decorated with pieces of glass, from Kleinlangheim. Next to that – some open-worked bronze discs, which were sewn onto pockets, colourful glass pendants, ● a special scale, numerous ornate combs which are still in very good condition, some whorls and a small reconstructed wooden box with the original bronze ornamentation, from Zeuzleben.

*Showcase 31:* Vessels from the Merovingian period (450–700 A.D.). Franconian glas beakers from the burial grounds in Kleinlangheim and Zeuzleben as well as ● a Franconian beaker and tumbler from Hellmitzheim. Bottom right – Franconian pots with lovely stamped decoration, made on a potter's wheel. To the left – hand-made local vessels, some of which are also decorated. In the centre – ● a cooking pot made out of lapis ollaris clearly bearing the marks of having stood over a fire, a bronze bowl and a reconstructed, turned

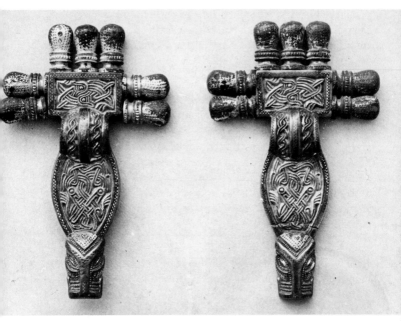

*Silver fibulas, found in Würzburg-Heidingsfeld,
early 7th century*

wooden beaker with ancient bronze rim. To the left – hand-made Thuringian pottery from Zeuzleben. Above that – Franconian pottery also made on a potter's wheel, and from Zeuzleben, a number of jugs, underneath – a toy jug, a bowl and a beaker.

*Showcase 32:* Grave of two horses and a dog dating from the Merovingian period (about 600 A.D.). In the burial grounds in Zeuzleben of the total of 68 graves, ten were for horses and dogs. Grave 45, which was recovered, preserved and brought to the Mainfränkisches Museum contains the sceletons of two beheaded horses and one dog. They were probably buried at the same time as their owner, a fact which clearly indicates that this man was wealthy and of high social standing. The custom of burying horses was dominant in the 6th century in those areas inhabited by Thuringians, who were famous for their horse breeding.

*Showcase 33:* Weapons and tools from the Merovingian period (450–700 A.D.). On the right – snaffles and other objects pertaining to the riding of horses. To the left – a pail, knives and scissors. Far left – different kinds of swords: a two-edged "Spatha" (long sword), a "Sax" (a one-edged short sword), "Franziska" (a Franconian throwing axe), blades of lances and shields, some with silver rivet heads. Special mention should be made of a gold-plated sword belt ornament whose clasp is decorated with an intricate animal design. These finds stem primarily from the burial site in Zeuzleben.

*Between showcase 33 and 34:* Arcades from "Teutleben" manor in the Domerschulstrasse, 12th century; and a "Christ Enthroned" from the "Burgkirche" (Fortress church), about 1180.

*Showcase 34:* Finds from a medieval dug well in Würzburg (13th/14th century). Numerous pieces of pottery, round handmade pots, vessels made on a potter's wheel (at the bottom of the showcase) as well as wooden objects such as, for example, nine wooden balls (for games), a comb, spindles, plates and bowls (at the top in the showcase). They are all in very good condition because they were cut off from the air by the wet earth in which they were enclosed. ● One thing especially worth mentioning is a one-handled beaker made from the wood of a pear tree and turned on a lathe, and also the fragment of the oldest European wooden flute (next to it, a modern functioning replica thereof).

*Showcase 35:* Medieval archeological finds from Würzburg and the surrounding areas (12th–15th century). Numerous ves-

*Wooden plates, stave-vessel and beaker, found in a Würzburg well, 13th century*

sels of shapes and sizes which differ, yet are typical for their particular period, a beer beaker with an elongated foot and the somewhat smaller "foot"-beakers. The round-bellied pots, deformed and discoloured by false treatment during burning in the potter's kiln, from the Kirschfurter Höfe should also be mentioned (bottom left). To the right – a collection of 150 coins, "Händel-Heller", found in the Reisgrubengasse in Würzburg, and 1147 specimens of the same coin along with the clay vessel they were found in near Röttingen, and also – a small toy figurine, made of clay, and depicting a little horse with its rider, from Würzburg-Heidingsfeld.

*Showcase 36:* Glasses excavated in the oldest part of Würzburg (13th–16th centuries). Top left ● a beaker made of colourless glass. The remaining glasses all stem from local workshops, including the "Nuppenbecher" (nipple-beakers) called "Krautstrünke" (cabbage stalks) because of their shape, and bowl-shaped glasses imitating the typical shape of 13th and 14th-century bowls which were made of wooden staves and willow sticks (showcase 34, top right).

*Würzburg master, tympanum with Enthroned Virgin and the two Saints John, about 1210.*

## The Lower South Bulwark (20)

houses romanesque and early gothic sculpture as well as numerous examples of medieval architectural sculpture, partially they are fragments found in the ruins of Würzburg in 1945.

● Stone baptismal font with a relief of the Baptism of Christ with His apostles, from the former Benedictine abbey in Neustadt am Main, from about 1150. In the window-recess on the left: "The Dream of St. Martin", a relief from a parclose also stemming from Neustadt, about 1150.

*Opposite the entrance:* ● Tympanum from the former church of St. Catharine in Würzburg, showing the Blessed Virgin enthroned between the two St. Johns, about 1210. On the same wall, various fragments of monumental statues: To the right of the recess, the damaged head of the statue of a youth, from the former Cistercian abbey church in Ebrach, fragment of a tombstone, about 1270. To the left of the recess, a knight's head from a grave stone of the former abbey church in Oberzell, about 1360.

The fragment in the window-recess stems from a Würzburg Madonna from about 1400. Next to the window-recess: Two tombstones of the 11th and 12th centuries with the so-called "Steigbügelkreuz", from the former Cathedral cemetery. In front of the window-recess, which contains an early gothic arched window from a Heidingsfeld house "zur Kemenate" (Bower House), stands a statue of the Virgin with Child from Retzbach am Main, from the 14th century.

Romanesque architectural sculpture, including, to the left of the entrance, a window arcade (about 1270) from the house "zum großen Löwen" (of the big lion) in the Herzogenstrasse/Dominikanergasse and also a palmette frieze from the former Church of St. James (about 1250) as well as an animal frieze (about 1130/40) and finally, (on the right-hand wall leading to the exit) ● four ornate capitals, from about 1130/40, from the old Stift Haug Church, which was razed in 1657.

*Near the exit*, by the stairs, on the left: Tombstone from Heiligenthal Monastery, about 1350. On the right: a votive column from Hopferstadt depicting the Crucifixion, about 1400.

## Wine Press Hall (21 a)
Originally the arsenal of the Fortress Marienberg, it is now devoted to objects concerned with the wine industry in Franconia. All kinds of festive occasions such as wine tastings and receptions etc. take place in this impressive hall. ● The magnificent wrought-iron gate at the entrance was made by Nikolaus Neeb in 1716 and originally stood at the entrance to the cellar of the arsenal. To the right of the entrance: The figure of a warrior, by Balthasar Esterbauer (1672–1728), from the former gate on the Old Main Bridge. The wall-paintings date

from the 18th century. Large monogram with the ducal hat of Franz Ludwig von Erthal, Prince-Bishop of Würzburg and Bamberg (1730–1795).

*Left:* ● Large oak wine presses of the baroque era from Franconian "wine-villages".

*Showcases on the walls near the wine presses:*

*1st showcase:* Faïence baroque jugs made in the manufactories located in Hanau, Frankfurt, Scherzheim, etc.

*2nd showcase:* Pewterware from the 17th to the 19th centuries, for example – pewter jugs of the various Franconian guilds.

*3rd showcase:* Goblets of the various guilds, salutation and drinking goblets. Top: ● The guild-symbol of the Locksmiths' Guild in Würzburg, an ornate key with incorporated goblet, was made by the Würzburg court locksmith, Johann Georg Oegg (1703–1782), in 1740. Center: A "Büttenmännchen", the goblet of the Würzburg Butchers' Guild, carved out of the wood of a grapevine, the silverwork done by the Würzburg court goldsmith, Bonifatius Wilhelm (1697–1766), in 1739. Furthermore, record books of the municipal wine-cellar in Würzburg and of the wine-cellar in Ochsenfurt, which belonged to the cathedral chapter (the latter book was known as the "Kauzenbuch" – the so-called "Owl Book").

*Showcases on the right near the gates:*

*Showcase 1:* Renaissance and baroque stoneware crockery. For example – Creussen jugs, ringed stoneware-jugs, a bottle in the shape of a book and stoneware-jugs from the Rhineland.

*Showcase 2:* Decorated glasses and goblets of the renaissance and baroque eras. For example – ● The "Imperial Eagle Tankards" of 1574, 1611, and 1652.

*Showcase 3:* Covered goblets, glasses and bottles of the baroque era with the crests of the various Prince-Bishops of Würzburg and of well-known Franconian families. Among other things, a humorous drinking vessel, a so-called "Non-

*Wine Press Hall*

nenbecher" (nun's cup) with a toast to the three best wines in Bacharach, Klingenberg and Würzburg, early 18th century.

*Showcase 4:* Goblets and glasses of the baroque era. For example – 18th century Venetian glasses, so-called "wing-glasses" and glasses with the crests of the various Prince-Bishops of Würzburg and of well-known Franconian fimilies.

*Showcase 5:* Decorated glasses as well as glasses with crests, all dating from the baroque era. For example: Large covered goblet bearing the crest of the former Provost of Würzburg Cathedral, Karl Friedrich Voit von Rieneck, Canon of Bamberg Cathedral and Provost of St. Burkard Church in Würzburg. Also, a covered goblet with the crest of Friedrich Karl von Schönborn, Prince-Bishop of Würzburg and Bamberg (1674–1746) and a covered goblet with the crest of Heinrich von Bibra, Prince-Bishop of Fulda (reigned from 1759–1788) as well as with Biblical scenes.

*Showcase 6:* Southern German and Thuringian baroque faïence jugs.

*Showcase 7:* Baroque faïence jugs. Jugs with the crests of various Würzburg Prince-Bishops, made in the manufactory in Hanau. Further – a jug in the shape of an innkeeper whose cocked hat forms the pouring spout, about 1765. Faïence jugs from Hanau bearing the emblems of various craftsmen's trades.

*Showcase 8:* Baroque covered goblets and glasses. This exhibit includes ● a goblet with the portrait Lothar Franz von Schönborn, Archbishop of Mainz and Prince-Bishop of Bamberg (1655–1729). A salutation glass with the crest of the same ruler.

*Showcase 10:* Glasses from the 19th century including a set of elegant drinking glasses made in the Bohemian glass factory in Harrachsdorf.

*Showcase 11:* Numerous wine glasses of different shapes and sizes, dating from the 18th and 19th centuries. A collection of different kinds of "Bocksbeutel" (the traditional bottle for Franconian wines).

*Showcase 12:* Tools and equipment for wine-pressing, including 18th century silver scales for weighing new wines. Stick belonging to the leader of a pilgrim-procession, carved out of the root of a grapevine, about 1770. Silver medallion marking the exceptional wine season in Franconia in 1779. Small wine press, about 1800.

*Near the gates:* Flags of Würzburg guilds of the Biedermeier period. Chests from Würzburg and Franconian guilds from the 17th to the 19th centuries. Especially noteworthy – Chest of the Shoemakers' Guild in Würzburg, 1649; ● richly decorated chest of the Würzburg Joiners' Guild, 1736. The chest of the Clothmakers' Guild in Schweinfurt is decorated with alabaster columns, 1707. The chest of the Fishers' Guild in Marktsteft features an intarsia with scenes taken from the life of a fisherman, 1833.

*Between the presses:* Escutcheons from the former "Ratstrinkstube". Large wrought-iron inn-signs. In the recesses on both sides of the last wine-press: Late gothic statues of St. Urban, the patron saint of vintners, the one on the left is from Pfaffendorf on the Franconian Saale (about 1500), and the one on the right is from Escherndorf on the Main, about 1520. And finally, a Franconian cart and equipment used for the grape harvest.

In a corner at the end of the hall, attached to the vaulting – the large stucco coat of arms of the Würzburg Prince-Bishop responsible for the construction of this building, Johann Philipp von Greiffenclau (1652–1719), 1715.

## Casemate (22)

of the Schönborn defences of 1649 with arms dating from the 17th to the 19th centuries; old flags and decorative targets.

## Schönborn Hall (21 b)

On the long wall: ● The ornate marble epitaphs of the Elector of Mainz and Prince-Bishop of Bamberg, Lothar Franz von Schönborn (1655–1729) (on the left) and of the Prince-Bishop of Würzburg and Bamberg, Friedrich Karl von Schönborn (1674–1746) (on the right). Both of these monuments were created by Johann Wolfgang von der Auwera in Würzburg in 1747. They were originally in Bamberg Cathedral, but were removed from there and deposited elsewhere. They were placed here in 1950/51 and have been on display in their present state since then. These two monuments are outstanding examples of Franconian sculpture of the baroque era. In front of them, two large statues of St. Kilian and St. Burkard by an unknown Bamberg master, about 1760, from the Baunach area. Pulpit from the former Prince-Bishops' chapel in the Upper Saltern in Bad Kissingen (later in Bad Bocklet), by the Würzburg court sculptor Johann Peter Wagner (1730–1809), 1772. By the same sculptor, two putti-groups with portraits of Albrecht Dürer (1471–1528) and von der Auwera, from the Court Garden of the Würzburg Residence, 1778/80. Further – a rococo sedan-chair, a so-called "Portchaise", with its original decorative painting, mid-18th century.

*Between the entrances:* Würzburg house-statues, damaged in 1945 when incendiary bombs sent the city up in flames. Some examples of these house-statues are "Mary Triumphant" by the Würzburg court sculptor, Claude Curé (1685–1745), about 1725, and "Mary and Joseph" by von der Auwera, about 1745.

*In the door-recesses:* Rococo confessional from Pfändhausen, about 1750, and a classicistic confessional from the former abbey in Oberzell, made by Johann Georg Winterstein (1743–1806), about 1785.

*Epitaph of Prince-Bishop Friedrich Karl von Schönborn, by Johann Wolfgang von der Auwera, 1747*

*Further:* The large banner of ● St. Kilian (measuring 6 metres), linen with remains of the original silk pattern. This is the oldest German field-standard still in existence. On St. Cyriac's Day (August 8th) in 1266 it was carried hanging from a pole on a special wagon in the battle on the Mühlberg near Kitzingen as the consecrated standard of the victorious Würzburg troops which were led by Berthold von Henneberg.

**Administrative Offices –**
*In the second courtyard (with fountain), on the left before the bridge.*

**Tours of the Fortress –**
*Through the second courtyard, across the bridge.*

**Tour round the outside of the Fortress –**
*In the second courtyard, through the last door on the right.*

**Restaurant – "Schänke zur Alten Wache" –**
*To the right of the Mainfränkische Museum*

*Pictures*
*Front cover: Adam and Eve, by Lucas Cranach the Elder, about 1515*
*Inside front cover: Adam (detail), by Tilman Riemenschneider, 1491/93*
*Inside back cover: St. Kilian's Banner, about 1266*
*Back cover: Eve (detail), by Tilman Riemenschneider, 1491/93*

Pictures furnished by:
Foto-Zwicker, Würzburg – inside front cover, inside back cover and back cover, page 7, 17, 23, 24, 27, 29, 31, 39, 43, 45, 51, 59, 63, 65, 67, 71, 73, 79, 83, 87, 95, 104, 106, 111
Foto-Gundermann, Würzburg – page 15, 21, 26, 35, 37, 57
Mainfränkisches Museum Archive – front cover, page 9, 11, 19, 47, 53, 69, 91, 99, 101, 103
Foto-Röder, Würzburg page 13